The Birthday List

Terri, we wish you a birthday filled with the gifts of friendship, fun and happiness. May today and all your days be amazing! Warm wishes and all life's best to you. Laura xx eSharp

The Birthday List

Laura Sharp and Oliver North

Editor: Julie Lewthwaite

Matador
9 Priory Business Park,
Wistow Road, Kibworth Beauchamp,
Leicestershire. LE8 0RX
Tel: 0116 279 2299
Email: books@troubador.co.uk
Web: www.troubador.co.uk/matador
Twitter: @matadorbooks

ISBN 978 1788032 964

British Library Cataloguing in Publication Data.
A catalogue record for this book is available from the British Library.

Printed and bound in the UK by TJ International, Padstow, Cornwall
Typeset in 11pt Calibri by Troubador Publishing Ltd, Leicester, UK

Matador is an imprint of Troubador Publishing Ltd

For everyone who has birthdays, this book is for you.

Contents

Introduction

A Birthday List is a list of things that you want to do before your next birthday. This book contains guidance and ideas to help you write your own Birthday List and get started on what may turn out to be the best year of your life so far.

You can begin this at any time and there are no limits as to what you can put on your list. The important thing is that it's written by you, for you.

The Birthday List is unique for three main reasons:

- *You have a date to work to...* The deadline for completing all the things on your Birthday List is your next birthday, as opposed to 'before you die' which, in most cases, is a rather unspecific timescale to work with! By having a clearly defined target date to help you focus, you'll be less likely to fall into the trap of thinking, *one day I'll do that...*but never actually getting around to it.

- *It's relevant to you now...* On your next birthday, you can write a new list containing new things that you want to do within the next year of your life. This encourages you to focus on what it's possible for you to achieve THIS YEAR. This is hugely beneficial as you will be able to take into account your current financial state and any commitments that need to be honoured whilst writing your Birthday List.

- *It's for everything you want to do...* **The Birthday List is designed for** aspirations of any size, no matter how great or small. It can allow you to keep focused on those bigger things that you want to do by breaking them down into smaller achievements. For example, attaining a black belt in Taekwondo may be something that you want to accomplish in your life, yet you may not be in a position to fulfil that goal this year. Instead, you can write things on your Birthday List that are realistic for this particular year, such as joining a Taekwondo club, learning a new pattern or moving up a belt. When this long-term goal becomes attainable (in this example, it will be the year that you are ready to take your black belt grading) you can then add this item to your Birthday List.

In years to come, your Birthday Lists could become sentimental keepsakes for your loved ones that show how you lived your life. They can be passed down to your children to remember you by and give them an insight into you as a person. Sharing your Birthday Lists will give your friends and family the opportunity to walk in your footsteps and experience some of the things that you've done. Your actions can inspire others to do things they've always wanted to do or try something amazing that they wouldn't have, had it not been for you.

Items on your Birthday List don't need to be monumental life-changing achievements. They can be small things, such as reading a book or throwing someone a surprise party. Both of these are valuable ways of spending your time if you take enjoyment from them. It's all about spending your time wisely, bringing positive energy into every experience and living the life you love.

Time spent happily is never wasted.

It is all too easy to forget about things you want to do. Everyday life takes over and if you're not careful, another year will have flown by all too quickly. The Birthday List is a simple, effective way to help you achieve more and get the most out of your time.

Your Birthday List can guide you to the achievement of your goals and act as a map to becoming a better version of yourself. When you know what you want out of life, you'll be surprised how many opportunities present themselves. This is the law of attraction at work. Open up your awareness to any suggestions, favourable circumstances, seemingly chance conversations and unexpected invitations that come your way. When your thoughts become your intentions they become a powerful attraction for the things that you seek.

> *"Keep your eyes open for blessings in disguise, they are everywhere."*
>
> (Katy Appleton)

So let's begin with some useful guidance in the construction of your Birthday List. Following this step-by-step guide will allow you the best chance of achieving your aims. It's all about feeling a sense of accomplishment, becoming a more successful person and having a lot of fun along the way.

Pick a list style

There are no rules governing what your Birthday List should look like, so choose a style that works for you. The first thing you will need to decide is whether you are handwriting your list or typing it. Then you need to pick a layout. You can use bullet points, colour coordination, a spider diagram, or any format that suits you.

Set the number of goals

The number of items on your Birthday List may vary from year to year depending on your personal circumstances. You have until your next birthday to accomplish as many things on your list as possible. You may feel that one objective per month is realistic or you might choose to match the number of items on your list to coincide with your current age (e.g. if you are 26 years old, compile a list of 26 things you want to do before you are 27). Maybe you can think of lots of things you want to do straight away, in which case don't hold back! It could prove beneficial to leave some space on your list so that you can keep adding to it throughout the year.

Mix it up

The lists contained within this book are full of ideas to help you write your own Birthday List. They have been broken down into the following eight chapters:

1. Family, friends and people
2. Health and well-being
3. Food and drink
4. Travel
5. Improving your mind
6. Cultivating interests
7. Money and work life
8. Just because you can

Ideally, try to put at least one thing from each of the above categories on your list to keep it varied and interesting.

"Variety's the very spice of life that gives it all its flavour."

(William Cowper)

Be really specific

Everything on your Birthday List must be specific enough to cross off once it has been achieved. If you use phrases such as 'do more…', 'improve at…', etc., you'll find that you won't know when to cross it off. For example, if you'd like to spend more time knitting, instead of writing 'knit more', specify what you'd like to make — put something like 'knit a jumper' or 'knit a tea cosy'. Changing this wording ever so slightly enables you to achieve your ultimate goal of doing more knitting, but it also means that once your specified item has been knitted you can cross it off your list.

Keep it achievable

In order to maintain your motivation it is important to set yourself achievable goals. This is beneficial, as making progress provides you with the inspiration to keep going. If you have an ambition to read the entire works of Shakespeare, for example, then perhaps break it down on your list. Research what the entire works of Shakespeare are first. This can be an item on your list in itself. Then every work of Shakespeare that you want to read can be itemised separately and ticked off your list once you've read it. It may take you a while to read them all, but by listing each of his works as separate items, every time you finish one you'll see your progress, giving you a sense of achievement. This strategy can be applied to any goal that you feel will take a long time to achieve.

Keep on track

If you have an item on your Birthday List that requires a regular activity, you may wish to adopt a method to help monitor your progress. For example, if you want to 'watch a different film every week' you can create a sub-list to detail the films that you watch alongside the dates that you watched them. You could even write them in your diary which will not only help you plan your week effectively but also provide you with a record of everything you have watched.

Find the time to fit it in

Finding time for your Birthday List will be the key to your success. Your time is very valuable and you should spend it as wisely as possible by doing things that are beneficial, interesting or fun. That said, this is your Birthday List and therefore the decision as to whether something qualifies for inclusion is completely up to you.

We all have exactly the same number of hours in our day.

Spending time on things that you feel are worthwhile gives you increased satisfaction. Consider ways you can maximise your time. Many people will spend upwards of an hour in their car each day, which could be time dedicated to learning a new language using an audiobook. You could also consider things that you can do whilst watching television, such as gentle exercise, sewing or making a friendship bracelet.

Be in control

Things like falling in love or having children by a certain age are not realistic goals as you have little or no control over them. They will only put an undesirable and unnecessary pressure on you.

You could apply the 'be really specific' and 'keep it achievable' guidance if you are looking for love and take positive steps towards increasing your chances of meeting someone special. There's no harm in adding something like 'join a dating site' or 'go to a singles cookery class' to your list, but know it might not lead to marriage and children.

Having a Birthday List will help you meet people you wouldn't have otherwise met. It might even make you a more appealing partner since you will be living a fulfilling life that you love.

"Happy people are beautiful. They become like a mirror and they reflect that happiness."

(Drew Barrymore)

It's no problem if some items on your list do rely on other people to achieve them, for example, playing a sport once a month. If you want to play badminton regularly, you will need a reliable partner and easy access to a court. This could prove an unrealistic aim if you are not part of a club.

Keep updating it

Your list shouldn't be a chore. Don't let it get tired or populated with things that you once wanted to do but no longer have the desire or motivation for. If there's something on your list that you don't want to do anymore, cross it through and replace it with something else. Don't feel bad about it, either! Refer to it often and keep it fresh and enjoyable.

Give your Birthday List a place in your life

The Birthday List has unlimited potential in terms of how it can benefit you, so harness this power and give it a special place to reside in your life. Perhaps display it inside your wardrobe, by your bed, inside your diary or organiser, folded into a bookmark, or set as the background on your PC. Give it the chance to enhance your life and position it where you will see it the most, so it can serve its purpose of reminding you of all the things you want to do before your next birthday.

Keeping all your Birthday Lists to look back on will help you to remember your achievements. They will allow you to reflect on your life knowing that you lived those years to the fullest, having acquired new skills, knowledge and experience.

"Sometimes it's the smallest decisions that can change your life forever."

(Keri Russell)

Family, Friends And People

People are your friends. Friends are your family.

Happiness and kindness are contagious. Therefore, surrounding yourself with happy and kind people can create an exceptionally positive environment. The more kindness and generosity we experience, the more inclined we become to do nice things for others. Connecting with people in a meaningful way enhances your life. Having a strong and loving circle of friends and family can, in some cases, even prolong it.

The Roseto Effect

In 1882, the first of over a thousand people from a small town in Italy immigrated to America. They settled in an area of the hills in Pennsylvania, which they named Roseto.

In 1961, physician Stewart Wolf observed that hardly anyone from Roseto under the age of sixty-five had been diagnosed with heart disease, which at that time in America was the leading cause of death in men under the age of sixty-five. Furthermore, he found that there was no suicide, no alcoholism, no drug addiction, no one on welfare and very little crime. The people of Roseto were predominantly dying of old age.

Wolf's investigation found that the people generally smoked heavily and many were struggling with obesity. He established, having also ruled out genetics and the geographic location of Roseto itself, that the reason for the low rate of heart disease was down to the community in which they thrived.

The Rosetan lifestyle involved a lot of neighbourly interaction, including talking in the streets and at work, cooking for one another and the populous church community. Elders were revered, housewives were respected and fathers ran the families, which often consisted of three generations living under one roof.

The Rosetans were healthy because of the world that they had created for themselves in a small town where people, family and friendship were greatly valued and community spirit was found in abundance on every street and in every home. Their story is proof of how family, friends and people can have an overwhelmingly positive effect on one another. Social connections and bonds between people have been shown to not only lower our risk of heart disease but also improve our immune systems and reduce mental decline in our old age.

Numerous good quality relationships mean you are more likely to be happy. Our friends and family can help us to feel loved, understood, appreciated and supported. This, in turn, allows us the opportunity to recognise our own characteristics, apply our natural talents and become the best version of ourselves.

It is through our friendships and interaction with others that we are best able to laugh, love and forgive. Life is all about moments. By sharing them with others, you can create special memories and unique bonds.

Did you know? During World War 2, seven-year-old Dorie Cooper visited her wounded uncle in hospital. Dorie asked her uncle to draw a picture of a bird, so he obliged and drew a robin for her. Dorie laughed at his drawing and told him that although it wasn't very good she would put the picture up in her room. Her uncle's spirits were lifted by Dorie's honesty and acceptance. Whenever Dorie came to visit from then on, the wounded soldiers held drawing contests to see who could produce the best bird pictures. Draw a Bird Day is celebrated worldwide on Dorie's birthday, 8 April.

Creating memories with people

- Organise a family get-together
- Throw a street party
- Start a giant conga line
- Host a fancy dress party
- Arrange a Eurovision Song Contest evening
- Host a pumpkin carving competition
- Organise a Christmas Party (have a 'mince off' and award a prize for the best mince pies)
- Get a pub quiz team together and sample different local quizzes
- Host a murder mystery night
- Go to a foam party
- Experience a silent disco
- Organise a brunch morning with your friends
- Take it in turns to experience each other's interests (invite your friends to join an activity that you enjoy doing regularly and vice versa)
- Go paintballing
- Arrange a go-kart racing experience
- Learn a dance with friends (e.g. Michael Jackson's 'Thriller')
- Choreograph a cheerleading song and routine
- Perform the haka as a team
- Join a flash mob

- Be part of a human pyramid
- Wear a 'free hug' T-shirt and see how many you can get
- Arrange a game of rounders in the park with your friends and family
- Organise a 'garden games' day (include a three-legged race, a wheelbarrow race or a game of horseshoes)
- Play Marco Polo in an outdoor swimming pool
- Host a crackers challenge (how many crackers can you eat in one minute without taking a drink?)
- Plan a family holiday
- Establish 'TV-free' nights at home
- Eat together as a family as often as possible

Did you know? Sharing a meal together is good for the spirit, the brain and the health of family members. Dinner is a time to relax, catch up on the day's events, recharge, laugh, tell stories and reconnect as a household. Research shows that children and teenagers who eat regular family meals do better academically and have greater self-esteem.

"The family that eats together, stays together."

(Unknown)

- Invent a secret handshake
- Draw each other on a night in
- Take a photo of yourself and a loved one at a place that is special to you both
- Complete a jigsaw puzzle with a loved one
- Hold a board games night
- Make a family video
- Take photos of your friends and family, put them in an album and date it as a keepsake of that year
- Create a family portrait

- Record a household answerphone message
- Listen to your grandparents' war stories
- Put together a 'Christmas Eve box', to be opened by the whole family, containing things to be used the night before Christmas (e.g. a new tree decoration, a game for everyone to play)
- Keep a child's belief in Father Christmas alive by showing them his flight path on the Internet on Christmas Eve

> **Did you know?** In 1961, during Soviet nuclear testing at the North Pole, a little girl wrote a letter to John F Kennedy asking if Santa Claus was OK. JFK wrote back to her and told her that he had spoken with Santa and that he was fine.

- Send your children on an Easter egg hunt
- Hold a competition for your nephews and nieces and award them each a certificate

"If you want your children to turn out well, spend twice as much time with them, and half as much money."

(Abigail Van Buren)

- Reconnect with an old friend
- Arrange a reunion with your school, college or university friends
- Get in touch with a teacher from your school years
- Tell someone you used to have a crush on them
- Go on a blind date
- Ask out a stranger
- Go speed dating
- Ride a tandem bicycle
- Have photos taken of you and a loved one in a photo booth
- Recreate your first date with your partner

- Take your partner back to the place you first met
- On 'date night' make an effort to dress to impress each other
- Celebrate International Kissing Day on 6 July
- Add a padlock to a 'love lock' bridge with your partner
- Renew your wedding vows

> **Did you know?** Wedding rings are traditionally placed on the fourth finger of the left hand because in ancient Roman times people believed it was the only finger from which a vein ran straight to the heart.

Ideas to make loved ones smile

- Buy a 'just because' present for someone (use the words, *'I saw this and thought of you'*)
- Give someone a friendship bracelet
- Cross-stitch a card for someone
- Give someone flowers for no reason
- Send a postcard to your grandparents every time you go on holiday
- Surprise a friend with a funny screen saver
- Make someone their very own compilation CD (or mixtape!)
- Contact a radio station and dedicate a song to someone
- Make a banner to support a friend who is taking part in a race
- Throw a surprise party for someone
- Arrange for every person in your friendship group to pick a flower from their garden and make a bouquet for someone you all love
- Buy someone a 'lucky pen' for their exam
- Win a giant stuffed animal for someone at the fair
- Give a child an astrological profile horoscope which identifies their character traits and explores their potential
- Create a mould of your baby's handprints
- Make a memory box to give to your child when they are older
- Pass on a family heirloom

- Do something in memory of someone who meant a lot to you (visit their favourite location or organise a get-together in their favourite pub)
- Tell your family members that you love them
- Create a 'then and now' family photograph (recreate a previous generation's photo)
- Frame your parents' or grandparents' wedding photos
- Pen a love letter
- Create a photo board for your soulmate displaying your life together
- Make your loved one breakfast in bed
- Run your partner a candlelit bubble bath when they get home from work
- Leave clues for your loved one to find when they walk through the door, leading them to a special gift or message
- King or Queen for a Day: dedicate a day just to your partner to spend however they want
- Establish a 'Birthday Bell' for a loved one (whenever they ring the bell on their birthday attend to their requests)
- Make birthday cards for the ones you love
- Create a family Christmas card
- Fold 1,000 origami cranes and give them to someone special

Did you know? According to ancient Japanese legend, a person who folds 1,000 origami cranes will be granted a wish by the gods. Today, a gift of 1,000 cranes is a symbol of hope and peace. Some stories believe you are granted eternal good luck, such as long life or recovery from illness or injury.

- Pen an 'open when...' letter to someone
- Write a letter to someone who has made a difference in your life
- Capture all your friends' and family members' birthdays, anniversaries and special occasions in a calendar so that you always remember them

- Apply for a congratulatory message from the monarch for a birthday or wedding anniversary
- Help someone else fulfil one of their goals in life

Kindness in the community

- Apply to do volunteer work
- Organise a litter pick in your local area
- Set up a monthly direct debit to a charity
- Get to know your neighbours, local shop assistants or pub bar staff
- Send a present to your postman at Christmas
- On a frosty morning, scrape the ice off your neighbour's car

"There are no such things as strangers, only friends we haven't met yet."

(Unknown)

- Take part in a survey the next time you are stopped in the street
- Show support to marathon runners or cyclists on race day
- Provide a great review for an establishment that made your experience special

- Leave a generous tip for excellent service
- Send your compliments to the chef
- Buy a round of drinks for the whole bar
- Spend time with an elderly neighbour and offer to help them with things they may struggle to do by themselves

Did you know? Nostalgia helps to protect us from loneliness. Studies have revealed that when people feel lonely they simultaneously increase their tendency to feel nostalgic as this allows them to feel more loved and therefore happier.

- Develop a deeper understanding of a physical or mental condition that someone you know has been diagnosed with (a little understanding goes a long way)
- Sponsor an underprivileged child
- Provide a foster home for an animal in need
- Register at 'BorrowMyDoggy' (it connects dog owners with local dog lovers for walks, sitting and holidays)
- Celebrate World Kindness Day on 13 November
- Go to a public address by a spiritual leader and try to learn from their teachings

"Compassion is a marvel of human nature, a precious inner resource and the foundation of our well-being and the harmony of our societies."

(The Dalai Lama)

"It's one of the greatest gifts you can give yourself, to forgive. Forgive everybody."

(Maya Angelou)

- Forgive someone
- Give blood

- Become a bone marrow donor
- Register as an organ donor

- Become a foster parent
- Visit an orphanage in another country with lots of toys for the children
- Gift a cow (it provides a family with milk and the dung can be used as fertiliser)

- Adopt an endangered animal
- Pay a compliment to everyone you speak to in a week
- Smile at every single person you encounter for a day
- Pay for the car behind you at a toll booth

Did you know? Generosity makes you happier and healthier. When you give to others it activates the area of the brain associated with pleasure, social connection and trust. It also boosts your immune system and helps fight stress. Studies reveal that generosity can spread from person to person. When one person behaves generously, it inspires others to do the same.

"No one ever became poor from giving."

(Anne Frank)

- Buy Easter eggs and/or Christmas presents for disadvantaged children
- Give money to a busker or street performer
- Take your old clothes to a charity shop
- Give a homeless person a meal or some warm clothes

"If you want happiness for an hour —
take a nap.
If you want happiness for a day —
go fishing.
If you want happiness for a year —
inherit a fortune.
If you want happiness for a lifetime —
help someone else."

(Chinese Proverb)

A must watch! *It's a Wonderful Life* (U) is a timeless Christmas classic about a compassionate yet suicidal man who is shown by his guardian angel what life would have been like for others if he had never existed.

Health And Well-Being

Health is a gift, take care of it.

Investing in your body, mind and spirit benefits all areas of your life, from work to your relationships. A conscious focus is required to be healthy because modern lifestyles generally do not promote this in themselves. Giving your body the right nutrients in a balanced diet, with regular exercise, allows you the best chance of gaining and maintaining optimum health. In turn, this enables you to do the things that you want to do.

There are no rules saying exercise must be painful or strenuous. The aim of this chapter is not to promote the gym or sports necessarily, but rather to encourage you to try something new or do a little bit more of something that's good for you.

Exercise is great for your mood as it decreases the stress hormone cortisol and increases endorphins, which are the body's natural feel-good chemicals. These are released in greater volume during and after physical activity, boosting your mood naturally. Just ten minutes of moderate exercise is enough to raise spirits and decrease fatigue.

Our bodies were meant to move. Regular exercise helps prevent diseases, increases stamina, strengthens your body, controls your weight and improves overall well-being. It can keep you looking and feeling younger throughout your entire life.

> Did you know? In March 2012, Tao Porchon-Lynch became the world's oldest yoga teacher at the age of 93.

"I don't believe in age. I believe in energy. Don't let age dictate what you can and cannot do."

(Tao Porchon-Lynch)

We're only as healthy as we are today and can all take steps towards improving or maintaining our fitness. You don't have to set yourself goals of great magnitude. Challenge yourself in line with your current state of health and build gently towards continuous improvement. This chapter contains ideas that can aid your well-being. The more you do, the easier it gets.

Regular activities to aid good health

> Did you know? Walking is one of the easiest ways to get more active, lose weight and become healthier. Regular walking has been shown to reduce the risk of chronic illnesses, such as heart disease, type 2 diabetes, asthma, stroke and some cancers. It can help you build stamina, burn excess calories, reduce stress and boost immune function.

"Walking is man's best medicine."

(Hippocrates)

- Complete all the walking routes from a particular guidebook
- Pledge to always take the stairs instead of the lift
- Embark on the 10,000 Steps Challenge
- Walk 1,000 miles in a year
- Try Earthing

> Did you know? Walking barefoot outside is an activity known as 'Earthing'. Growing research suggests that the Earth's surface contains natural healing energy and physically connecting to it has significant benefits for your health. Studies, published in the book *Earthing*, by Clinton Ober, show that among other advantages it improves sleep and reduces pain and inflammation, which are at the root of many health disorders.

- Go for a walk in a forest once a month

> Did you know? 'Shinrin-yoku' is a Japanese term developed in the 1980s that means 'forest bathing'. Researchers have developed credible, science-based literature on the health benefits of spending time in a forest. These include a boosted immune system, reduced blood pressure, reduced stress, improved mood, accelerated recovery from surgery or illness, increased energy level and improved sleep.

*"You didn't come into this world.
You came out of it, like a wave
from the ocean.
You are not a stranger here."*

(Alan Watts)

- Go jogging twice a week (keep a record of your times to keep you motivated)
- Join a running club
- Hire a personal trainer
- Go mountain biking
- Enrol on a boot camp training programme
- Learn a calisthenics routine (exercises using just your bodyweight that you can do anywhere)
- Complete a new exercise video
- Attend a session at a hot yoga studio
- Experience an aerial fitness class (mid-air workout using hanging silk hammocks)
- Try out every single type of exercise class provided by your local gym

"Wow. I really regret that workout."

(No one ever)

- Join a local sports team
- Take up a racket sport
- Attend regular dance classes and learn at least one new routine
- Study a martial art and obtain a belt
- Meditate

Did you know? Benefits of regular meditation include improvements to sleep patterns, memory, brain function and metabolism. It also strengthens the immune system, promotes healing, reduces stress levels, leads to better and more fulfilling relationships and increases happiness. Research, published in the book *Mindfulness* by Professor Mark Williams and Dr Danny Penman, has shown that daily practice over a period of just eight weeks is enough for parts of the brain associated with happiness, empathy and compassion to become stronger and more active.

Did you know? Tibetan monks practicing an advanced form of meditation known as 'g-Tummo' can raise their core body temperature at will.

Physical achievements

- Perform a diving board trick
- Perfect a swimming stroke
- Learn how to tumble turn in a swimming pool
- Swim across a lake (if swimming is permitted and you have support)

Success story: On 4 July 2006, David Walliams swam the English Channel for Sport Relief. Five years later, in September 2011, Walliams surpassed this achievement when he swam a 140-mile section of the River Thames. During his swim he experienced symptoms of hypothermia, encountered severe stomach problems due to the bacteria in the Thames, and also suffered a torn disc. Upon finishing his eight-day swim he had raised over £1million for charity.

> *"No matter how slow you go, you are still lapping everybody on the couch."*

(Unknown)

- Try surfboarding
- Master skiing to an advanced standard and tackle a black ski run
- Run a mile in under ten minutes
- Sign up for a fun run (e.g. The Color Run or Electric Run)

> Did you know? There's a competitive sport called 'joggling' that combines jogging and juggling. People who do this are called jogglers.

- Take part in a hashing event, where 'hares' (runners who lay a trail) are followed by a pack of 'hounds' (other runners) who attempt to catch them before the trail ends
- Go orienteering
- Compete in a tower running event
- Run a half-marathon
- Compete in the London Marathon

> Success story: On 27 July 2009, the comedian and actor Eddie Izzard started his challenge of running a marathon every day for seven weeks, taking only Sundays off (43 marathons in 51 days). He ran across the UK through the cities of London, Cardiff, Belfast and Edinburgh. He completed his final marathon on 15 September 2009, having covered more than 1,100 miles. Eddie started this great feat with only five weeks' training and no significant prior history of running.

> *"We can all do more than we think we can."*

(Eddie Izzard)

- Develop a six-pack
- Punch, chop or kick a wooden board in half
- Touch your toes
- Master a headstand
- Walk on your hands
- Perform a cartwheel
- Do the splits
- Learn to backflip
- Perfect a trampolining move
- Scale an indoor climbing wall
- Bend backwards and crawl down the wall with your hands
- Achieve 100 'keepie uppies' with a football
- Score more than 500 runs in a cricket season
- Shoot 20 basketball hoops consecutively
- Perform ten consecutive pistol squats
- Complete the 200 Squats Challenge
- Do 50 sit ups in one go
- Achieve 30 minutes of hula-hooping
- Embark on a 30-day fitness challenge (e.g. the 30 Day Burpee, Jump Rope or Tricep Dip Challenge)
- Complete the 404040 Plan (a fitness plan specifically designed for people over the age of 40)
- Do the 'Bring Sally Up' Push-up Challenge

> Did you know? On 27 November 1993, The UK's Paddy Doyle entered the Guinness World Records for the most one-arm push-ups in one hour, achieving 1,868.

- Complete the INSANITY workout
- Take part in an obstacle course race (e.g. Tough Mudder, Spartan Race)

- Apply to compete in a physically challenging TV programme (e.g. *Ninja Warrior UK*)
- Cycle from Land's End to John O'Groats
- Complete an Ironman triathlon

"I'm trying to send a message to anyone, that, actually, if I can do it, then anyone can do it."

(Sean Conway)

- Complete the Coast to Coast Walk
- Trek the Nene Way
- Walk the Thames Path Trail
- Tackle the South West Coast Path
- Reach the summit of the top ten highest peaks in Great Britain
- Climb a famous mountain
- Complete the 24-hour Three Peaks Challenge (Ben Nevis, Scafell Pike and Snowdon)
- Conquer one of the world's seven summits

"*PAIN IS TEMPORARY! It may last for a minute, or an hour, or a day, or even a year. But eventually it will subside and something else will take its place. If I quit, however, it will last forever.*"

(Eric Thomas)

Other beneficial health experiences

- Quit smoking
- Have an alcohol-free month
- Watch no television for a month

> **Did you know?** Heavy watching of television is linked with lower life satisfaction, higher material aspirations and higher anxiety. Aside from the obvious side effects of weight gain and lethargy, watching television also slows down brain activity.

- Research your family medical history
- Book in for a health assessment
- Visit a chiropractor for a spinal and postural assessment

- Try colon hydrotherapy
- Experience an acupuncture session
- Research colour therapy
- Receive an ear candling treatment
- Experience Reiki by a trained therapist
- Receive an aura and chakra cleanse
- Enjoy a hot stone or lava shell massage
- Book a seaweed wrap treatment
- Receive an Indian head massage
- Experience reflexology
- Explore healing sound frequencies
- Go on a yoga retreat
- Attend a Mind Body Spirit Well-being festival
- Make improvements to the quality of your sleep
- Research the benefits of humour therapy

A must watch! *Patch Adams* (PG-13), starring Robin Williams, is based on the true story of a medical student in the 1970s who treats patients using humour. A quote from the film is, *'Remember laughing? Laughter enhances the blood flow to the body's extremities and improves cardiovascular function. Laughter releases endorphins and other natural mood-elevating and pain-killing chemicals, improves the transfer of oxygen and nutrients to internal organs. Laughter boosts the immune system and helps the body fight off disease, cancer cells, as well as viral, bacterial and other infections. Being happy is the best cure of all diseases!'*

- Treat yourself to a health spa
- Research, develop and implement a good skincare regime
- Incorporate dry skin brushing into your daily routine
- Cut back on the frequency of your hair washing (dermatologists and stylists agree that there's little reason to shampoo every day)
- Keep a food diary for two weeks to analyse your eating habits

- Eat five servings of fruit and vegetables every day
- Research the superfoods and incorporate at least five of them into every weekly food shop
- Drink one homemade juice or smoothie every day for a month
- Detox for seven days
- Complete a three-day fast (do this safely and keep properly hydrated)

Did you know? Scientists at the University of Southern California have discovered evidence to suggest that fasting for three days can regenerate the entire immune system. The award-winning researcher and professor, Valter Longo, says of fasting, *'There is no evidence at all that fasting would be dangerous, while there is strong evidence that it is beneficial'.*

- Get your cholesterol level checked
- Cut out something that's unhealthy from your diet completely
- Drink more water (set yourself a healthy daily target)
- Cut sugar out of your diet for a week

Did you know? Refined sugar has no nutritional value, just empty calories. Everything beneficial, including vitamins and minerals, are removed during the refining process.

"*No matter how much money you spend on amazing skin creams, you simply can't undo the cellular damage that sugar causes from the inside.*"

(*Eat. Nourish. Glow.* by Amelia Freer)

- Lose 'X' amount of weight (research this topic carefully and find a healthy and sustainable solution to suit your lifestyle)

A must watch! **'Teach every child about food', presentation by TED Prize winner Jamie Oliver**
'I wish for your help to create a strong, sustainable movement to educate every child about food, inspire families to cook again and empower people everywhere to fight obesity.'
(Jamie Oliver)

Food And Drink

Our need for food and drink is a mutual bond that has been bringing people together since the dawn of time. The cuisines of today have been developed from generations of family teachings and social experiences, handed down through the ages. Food and drink brings a wonderful opportunity for sharing wisdom and nourishment with others.

This section contains ideas for developing your palate and expanding your culinary horizons. The Birthday List is all about new things and because of the frequency with which we eat and drink, every day presents an excellent opportunity to accomplish some goals.

We are fortunate in the Western hemisphere that we have an abundance of food and drink readily available to us from all over the world, all year round. There's always something new or amazing to learn in terms of both the production and preparation of food and drink. Furthermore, there's no need to travel thousands of miles to seek it out. New culinary delights and tasty experiences can be found inside your nearest supermarket, restaurant or cookbook.

"Food is essential to life, therefore make it good."

(S. Truett Cathy)

33

Food is one of the easiest, most accessible ways to challenge your comfort zone. Embracing different foods with an open mind teaches you new perspectives. Varying your diet through self-imposed restrictions, such as vegetarianism, encourages you to think about what you are eating and perhaps venture towards things you have never experienced before.

Savoury delights

- Bake a loaf of bread
- Make your own butter
- Try twenty different types of cheese
- Make your own pâté
- Jar your own relish, chutney or jam (perhaps using home-grown plants)
- Learn how to make different types of pastry
- Try black pudding
- Poach an egg
- Make a cheese soufflé
- Prepare a full English breakfast
- Make a soup
- Create your own pizza
- Make an omelette or frittata
- Prepare a meal using up all your leftovers
- Have a picnic
- Make your own houmous or guacamole dip
- Learn to roll sushi
- Cook a roast dinner with all the trimmings
- Prepare an authentic curry
- Learn the different types of pasta
- Make a casserole with homemade dumplings
- Try a traditional Scottish haggis
- Take part in 'Welsh Rarebit Day' on 3 September
- Enter a Christmas ham competition
- Taste an exotic meat
- Celebrate 'National BBQ Month' in May
- Try the London-born dish, jellied eels
- Eat ten different types of fish or seafood

- Go deep sea fishing and eat your catch
- Shuck an oyster
- Eat lobster

Did you know? In the Victorian era, lobsters were considered the 'cockroaches of the sea' and they bred in such abundance around Britain's coastline that they were fed to prisoners and orphans, or ground up for fertiliser.

- Eat a hot chilli pepper
- Try a fresh coconut straight from a tree
- Go vegetarian for a month

Did you know? Scientific bone analysis found that the gladiators that fought in the Colosseum in ancient Rome mainly lived on a vegetarian diet rich in carbohydrates.

- Take on the Veganuary challenge

"Going vegan is the best thing any individual can do for the animals, the planet and your health. What are you waiting for?"

(Jasmijn de Boo)

- Compile a folder of family recipes or your tried and tested favourites
- Learn to make a dish so well that it becomes your signature dish
- Open a cookbook at a random page and follow the recipe on it (regardless of whether you think you'll like it — it might surprise you!)
- Work your way through every recipe in a particular cookery book
- Eat at least one local dish from every place you visit
- Try everything on the BBC's list of '50 things to eat before you die'
- Tuck into a bento box (Japanese lunch box)
- Learn to eat with chopsticks
- Order something that you have never tried before from a takeaway menu
- Try at least one new food every fortnight
- Eat a different cuisine every night for a week
- Enrol in a cookery class

Sweet treats

- Learn the best way to cut up a mango
- Taste 50 different fruits

> Did you know? The fruit salad tree is a tree that grows up to six different types of fruit on the same tree. You could keep your own fruit salad tree as an idea for your Birthday List...

- Make a blueberry fool
- Try five types of rare or expensive chocolate
- Attend a chocolate making lesson
- Make fudge
- Learn to make your favourite biscuits
- Create a homemade ice cream sundae
- Make your own popcorn
- Learn to make three different types of meringue
- Make a crème brûlée

- Perfect a tiramisu recipe
- Try a slice of Black Forest gâteau
- Make a cheesecake
- Serve fresh peach flambé with crepes
- Bake a crumble or a pie
- Try bread and butter pudding
- Make scones and serve them for afternoon tea
- Bake five different types of cake
- Make a batch of decorated cupcakes
- Create your own sugar flowers to decorate a cake with
- Make a novelty cake (e.g. a chess cake, Guinness cake)
- Make a Christmas pudding
- Build a gingerbread house
- Celebrate Shrove Tuesday by making pancakes
- Eat toasted marshmallows around a campfire

Down the hatch

- Brew your own beer
- Make sloe gin
- Visit an establishment rated in the *Good Pub Guide*
- Learn how to make your favourite cocktail
- Try a classic cocktail you have never tried before
- Attend a wine tasting course
- Drink a £500+ bottle of champagne
- Sample all the different types of milk available in your local supermarket
- Try cactus water
- Sample every type of coffee available on the menu at your local coffee shop (same sitting not recommended!)
- Research how to make the perfect cup of English breakfast tea
- Attend a Japanese tea ceremony
- Experience ten different types of tea that you have never tried before

> Did you know? The act of tea drinking is one of the great British traditions, yet it hasn't always been. In the Middle Ages, beer or ale was consumed daily by many people, including children. English sailors even received a ration of eight pints of beer per day! Tea first came to England in the 17th century and by the mid-18th century had replaced beer as the national drink.

Dining

- Visit a restaurant recommended in the *Good Food Guide*
- Eat at one of the world's best restaurants
- Dine in a Michelin star restaurant
- Visit a restaurant that is run by a celebrity chef
- Eat in five different restaurants within your local area that you have never been to before
- Host a dinner party *Come Dine with Me* style
- Have a Mexican night with quesadillas (and tequila!)
- Host a Spanish tapas evening
- Hold a cheese and wine night
- Go to a 'Miracle Fruit Party'

> Did you know? The miracle fruit is a plant native to West Africa which has a unique effect on taste buds. It causes bitter and sour foods to temporarily taste sweet, with the effects lasting up to two hours. Recently, the fruit has become popular in food tasting events, where sour and bitter foods are consumed in order to experience the dramatic change in taste.

- Prepare a six-course meal
- Experience al fresco dining

- Eat fresh fish and chips by the sea
- Dine in an undersea restaurant
- Visit a 'dining in the dark' restaurant
- Dine in the sky (a dining experience held fifty metres up in the air)
- Enjoy afternoon tea at a famous location (e.g. The Ritz, Claridge's)
- Order an expensive truffle from a menu
- Try snails or frog legs in a French restaurant

"If more of us valued food and cheer and song above hoarded gold, it would be a merrier world."

(J.R.R. Tolkien)

Travel

There are so many new smells, sounds, sights, tastes, cuisines, beverages, stories, buildings, people, art, history, flora, fauna, and much, much more, waiting to be discovered on this incredible planet. By travelling and experiencing new surroundings you can't help but appreciate life more. By making the decision to travel to a new place, you instantly begin creating memories and experiencing new things. To go to another country, or even somewhere nearby that you have never visited, will open your mind to new ideas and perceptions.

"To travel is to live."

(Hans Christian Andersen)

A journey that once would have taken several months can now be made in less than twenty-four hours. Furthermore, travel doesn't have to be unaffordable. With low cost airlines and cheap accommodation at your disposal, there is no reason why you can't get away on a modest budget. There really is nothing to stop you.

Travelling can help you to realise the good points about the place you are from, teaching you to value aspects of your hometown that you may have previously taken for granted. There are billions of people on the planet, many of them living in varied and often difficult conditions. Local people, as much as the climate or scenery, can provide you with new perspectives, which is what travelling is all about.

Travelling can teach you what is of greatest importance to you. In the routine of day-to-day life it's easy to go a long time without thinking about what you're doing and where you are going. A trip abroad can remedy this quickly — you can escape from routine and allow yourself the opportunity to reflect on your life and situation. It's not important how far you travel or what you do when you arrive. What is important is to get out there and go somewhere new.

"Better to see something once than to hear about it a thousand times."

(Asian Proverb)

The British Isles

- Explore your neighbourhood on foot
- Visit a nearby place that you have never been to before
- See or do the top ten things in your local area
- Visit every country in the British Isles
- Go to Lerwick in Shetland to celebrate Up Helly Aa Day
- Complete the North Coast 500
- Pick up the Malt Whisky Trail in the Scottish Highlands
- Go to Urquhart Castle (and look for the Loch Ness monster!)
- Watch the Highland Games in Braemar
- Plunge into the River Forth for the Loony Dook on 1 January
- Go to the Edinburgh Fringe Festival
- Celebrate St Patrick's Day in an Irish bar
- Visit Adare, often referred to as Ireland's prettiest village
- Drive the Ring of Kerry
- Kiss the Blarney Stone (it is said to grant you with the 'gift of the gab')

- Visit St David's Cathedral in Pembrokeshire
- Complete a 'Waterfall Country' walking trail in the Brecon Beacons National Park
- Take in the mountain air in Snowdonia
- Go to the Holy Island of Lindisfarne in North East England
- See the Angel of the North sculpture in Gateshead
- Tackle Striding Edge on the mountain of Helvellyn in the Lake District
- Go to Blackpool Pleasure Beach
- Experience a ghost walk in York
- Go to the International Antiques and Collectors Fair in Nottinghamshire
- Walk around the Hambleton Peninsula in Rutland Water
- Abseil down the National Lift Tower in Northampton
- Hire a canal boat for a weekend on the Norfolk Broads
- Watch a Shakespeare play in Stratford-Upon-Avon
- Paddle in River Windrush at Bourton-on-the-Water in the Cotswolds
- See the autumn leaves at Westonbirt Arboretum in Gloucester
- Dress for the annual World Pooh Sticks Championships in Oxfordshire
- Go to the Henley Royal Regatta
- Spend a day seeing as many of London's blue plaques as you can (you could download the app that shows the locations of these famous signs that honour notable people in history)
- Recreate The Beatles *Abbey Road* album cover at the famous London zebra crossing
- See the Changing of the Guards at Buckingham Palace
- Join a Beefeater Tour of the Tower of London
- See original artwork in the streets of Bristol by Banksy
- Go to the Roman baths in the city of Bath
- Visit Stonehenge
- Navigate your way through the Longleat Hedge Maze
- Go to Corfe Castle in Dorset, which dates to the 11th century
- Eat a Cornish pasty in Cornwall
- Visit Canterbury Cathedral in Kent
- Travel through the Channel Tunnel

- Bathe in the Blue Lagoon geothermal spa at Grindavik, Iceland
- Visit the Icelandic Phallological Museum, home to the world's largest display of penises
- Witness Aurora Borealis (the Northern Lights)
- Visit the Norwegian Ice Music Festival in Geilo
- Go to the Pulpit Rock in Norway
- Stay at the Icehotel in Sweden
- Visit Father Christmas and enjoy a reindeer-drawn sleigh ride in Lapland
- Stay in the Igloo Village in Finland
- Attend the Mobile Phone Throwing World Championships in Savonlinna, Finland
- Go to the Hermitage Museum in St Petersburg, Russia
- Visit the Red Square in Moscow
- Ride the Trans-Siberian Railway
- See *The Motherland Calls* statue in Volgograd, Russia
- Enter the Upside Down House in Szymbark, Poland
- Go to Auschwitz concentration camp in Poland
- Visit the Sedlec Ossuary ('The Bone Church') in the Czech Republic
- Attend the Berlin Tattoo Convention
- Walk around Nuremberg's Christmas market in Germany
- Drink beer at the Oktoberfest in Munich
- Tour the Neuschwanstein Castle in Bavaria
- Go extreme camping in Pfronten in Germany
- Drive on the German autobahn
- Visit the Anne Frank House in Amsterdam
- Complete the Somme Remembrance Trail
- See the Mona Lisa at the Louvre in Paris
- Walk to the top of the Eiffel Tower
- Visit Normandy's D-Day beaches and museums
- Go to the Chartres Cathedral in France
- Drink Champagne in the Champagne wine region of France
- Have a flutter in Monte Carlo
- Go to the Baby Jumping Festival in Spain (described as one of the world's strangest festivals)

- Attend the Running of the Bulls in Pamplona in Spain
- Go to La Mercè Festival in Barcelona
- Throw tomatoes at La Tomatina festival in Valencia
- Experience the nightlife in Ibiza
- Visit the Stone House near Guimarães, Portugal
- Take in the panoramic views in the Alps
- Have a ride on the Big Pintenfritz in Switzerland (the longest toboggan run in Europe)
- Dip into a cheese fondue in Zurich
- Watch a rendition at the Staatsoper (Vienna State Opera house)
- Ride on a gondola in Venice
- Attend the annual Venice Carnival
- Experience the Cervia International Kite Festival in Italy
- Have your photo taken 'propping up' the Leaning Tower of Pisa
- Go to the Calcio Storico ('Historic Football') annual tournament held in Florence
- See the *Adoration of the Magi* by Leonardo da Vinci in the Uffizi Gallery
- Visit the Colosseum in Rome
- See the Sistine Chapel in the Vatican City
- Visit the partially-buried Roman town of Pompeii in Italy
- Attend 'Exit', the summer music festival in Serbia
- Visit Bran Castle ('Dracula's Castle') in Romania
- See the Parthenon in Greece
- Visit the Acropolis of Athens
- Go to a Greek Island
- Ride a hot air balloon over the Cappadocian landscape in Turkey
- Tour Hagia Sophia in Istanbul
- Take a trip on the Venice Simplon-Orient-Express
- Visit five capital cities in Europe

Africa

- Go trekking in the Atlas Mountains
- Shop in the souks of Marrakech
- Stargaze at the foot of the Merzouga Dunes in the Sahara Desert

- Go to the Cairo Museum and see the gold mask of Tutankhamun
- Visit the pyramids in Egypt
- See the Great Sphinx of Giza
- Cruise down the Egyptian Nile
- Take a camel ride up to Mount Sinai (where Moses was said to have received the Ten Commandments)
- Spot crocs at the Kachikally Crocodile Pool in The Gambia
- Go hiking in the Simien Mountains National Park in Northern Ethiopia
- See mountain gorillas in Uganda
- Watch the flamingos at Lake Nakuru National Park in Kenya
- Go on safari at the Maasai Mara National Reserve
- Journey to Ngorongoro Crater in Tanzania
- Visit Serengeti National Park
- Set foot on Mount Kilimanjaro
- Go diving in Lake Malawi
- Swim in the Devil's Pool at the top of Victoria Falls waterfall
- Take a 'mokoro' ride in the Okavango Delta in Botswana (the world's largest inland delta)
- Go rustic cave camping at Spitzkoppe in the Namib desert
- Visit the Fish River Canyon in Namibia
- Stroll through Municipal Market in Maputo, Mozambique
- Go to the Kruger National Park
- Learn of our ancestry at The Cradle of Humankind (the 'birthplace of humanity')
- Visit Table Mountain in South Africa
- Go to Cape Point, where the Indian and Atlantic Oceans meet
- Spot lemurs in Madagascar
- Experience the beaches of the Seychelles

Did you know? Africa is the only continent in the world that lies in all four hemispheres — Northern, Southern, Eastern and Western. This is because both the equator and prime meridian run through it.

- Visit the Holy Land
- Go to Bethlehem in Israel (the birthplace of Jesus)
- Visit Petra in Jordan
- Float in the Dead Sea
- Go to Ferrari World in Abu Dhabi
- Stay in the 7-star Burj Al Arab hotel in Dubai
- See the Sea of Stars in the Maldives
- Visit an Indian ashram
- Experience a Holi Festival of Colours in India
- Go to the 'Golden Temple' at Amritsar in India (the spiritual centre for the Sikh religion)
- See the Taj Mahal
- Visit Varanasi (regarded as the spiritual capital of India)
- Trek to Everest base camp in the Himalayas
- Go to the 'Tiger's Nest' Monastery in Bhutan
- Visit the Bagan Temples in Myanmar

Did you know? Between the 11th and 13th centuries, over 10,000 Buddhist temples, pagodas and monasteries were built in the Bagan plains. The remains of over 2,200 temples and pagodas have survived to this present day.

- Island hop around Thailand
- Attend the Monkey Buffet Festival in Lopburi
- Visit the world's largest solid gold Buddha statue in Wat Traimit temple, Bangkok
- Go to Angkor Wat in Cambodia
- See the Kuala Selangor fireflies in Malaysia
- Ride on the 165-metre tall Singapore Flyer
- Drink the famous Singapore Sling cocktail at Raffles Hotel
- Visit the Gunung Mulu National Park in Borneo
- Go to Lhasa (the centre of Tibetan Buddhism)

- See the Leshan Giant Buddha in China
- Take a boat along the Yangtze River
- Travel on the Beijing-Shanghai High-Speed Railway
- Walk a section of the Great Wall of China
- Experience a Chinese Lantern Festival
- Go to the Harbin International Ice and Snow Festival
- Visit the Venetian Macao
- Experience the Symphony of Lights on the Star Ferry in Hong Kong
- Shop at the night markets in Taiwan
- Visit the Love Land theme park on Jeju Island
- Play in the mud at the Boryeong Mud Festival in Seoul
- Go to Hadaka Matsuri (commonly known as the Naked Festival) in Japan
- See the Tranquil Zen Garden of Kyoto
- Visit Japan when the cherry blossom trees are in full bloom

Did you know? Japan consists of over 6,800 islands.

Oceania

- Stay in an overwater bungalow in Bora Bora
- Bathe in the 'Coca Cola' Lake on Karikari Peninsula, New Zealand
- Kayak through the Bay of Islands
- Go fishing in the Kai Iwi Lakes
- Hike amongst the trees and waterfalls in the Waitakere Ranges
- Book a 'bach' on Waiheke Island, east of Auckland
- Dig your own spa pool in the sand at Hot Water Beach, Coromandel
- Take a tour of the Hobbiton Movie Set in Matamata (home of 'Middle-earth' from *The Lord of the Rings* movies)
- See the geysers, bubbling mud pools and hot thermal springs in Rotorua
- Attend the Tamaki Māori Village cultural night
- Skydive over Lake Taupo
- Go skiing in Mount Tongariro National Park

- Travel from Hawkes Bay to Marlborough on the Classic New Zealand Wine Trail
- Go whale watching in Kaikoura
- Attend the Hokitika Wildfoods Festival
- Explore Franz Josef Glacier
- Take an alpine walk in Mount Cook National Park
- Paraglide over Lake Wanaka
- Soak up the scenery at Milford Sound
- Go flyboarding on Lake Wakatipu in Queenstown
- Take the Canyon Swing over the Shotover River
- See a selection of Australia's 'Big Things' (e.g. The Big Lobster, The Big Rocking Horse)
- Snorkel off Australia's Great Barrier Reef
- Experience the secluded beaches of the Whitsunday Islands
- Camp on Fraser Island, off Australia's eastern coast
- Cuddle a koala bear and hand feed kangaroos at Lone Pine Koala Sanctuary in Brisbane
- Scuba dive around the shipwrecked *SS Yongala* off the coast of Queensland
- Spend Christmas Day on Bondi Beach in Sydney
- Climb Sydney Harbour Bridge
- Go trekking in the Blue Mountains
- Drive Australia's Great Ocean Road
- Talk to someone standing 450ft away at the other end of the Barossa Reservoir ('The Whispering Wall') as though they were right next to you
- Visit the colourful Bay of Fires in Tasmania
- Attend the annual Tunarama Festival in Port Lincoln
- Walk around Uluru ('Ayers Rock')
- See Wave Rock in Western Australia

The Americas

- Visit the Tatshenshini-Alsek Provincial Wilderness Park in Alaska
- Ride the Rocky Mountaineer train through the Rocky Mountains
- Hang from Toronto's CN Tower in Canada

- See Niagara Falls
- Tour the *HMS Titanic* wreckage at the bottom of the Atlantic Ocean (this is not cheap!)
- Go to the Heidelberg Project in Detroit, Michigan
- Ride all of the roller coasters at Ohio Cedar Point Amusement Park
- Attend the Groundhog Day ceremonies in Punxsutawney
- Visit Fallingwater, a house built over a waterfall, in Pennsylvania
- Run up the 'Rocky Steps' in Philadelphia
- Go to the Gettysburg Battlefield
- Visit the Salem Witch Museum
- Ferry across to the Statue of Liberty
- Visit the Guggenheim Museum in New York
- Go ice skating in Central Park at Christmas
- Visit the 9/11 Memorial at the World Trade Center
- Tour the White House in Washington D.C.
- Hike a section of the Appalachian Trail
- Go to Walt Disney World Resort
- Visit the Everglades National Park in Florida
- Join the celebrations at Mardi Gras in New Orleans
- Experience a cowboy ranch in Texas
- Participate in the annual Texas SandFest
- Go to Dollywood in Tennessee (Dolly Parton's theme park)
- Attend the Grand Ole Opry in Nashville
- Visit Graceland in Memphis
- Go to a real blues bar in Chicago
- Do Route 66
- Shop at the Mall of America in Minnesota
- See the Crazy Horse Memorial in South Dakota
- Go to Mount Rushmore National Memorial
- See Carhenge in Nebraska (replica of England's Stonehenge formed from vintage cars)
- Visit Mesa Verde National Park in Colorado
- Bungee jump off Royal Gorge Bridge
- Experience horseback riding in Swan Valley, Montana
- See the Old Faithful geyser at Yellowstone National Park
- Stare up at one of the world's tallest trees in Redwood National Park

- Make your own wine in Napa Valley in California
- Walk across the Golden Gate Bridge in San Francisco
- Visit Yosemite National Park
- Cruise down Highway 1 in a convertible
- Go inner tubing down the Kern River in California
- Experience Hollywood in Los Angeles
- Walk along the Santa Monica Pier
- Visit Joshua Tree National Park
- Experience the heat of Death Valley in summer
- Attend the Burning Man festival in Nevada
- Visit the outskirts of Area 51
- Go to a pool party in Las Vegas
- Hike in the Grand Canyon
- Go to Roswell UFO Museum in New Mexico
- Take a helicopter tour over the Hawaiian island of Kauai (featured in *Jurassic Park*)
- Visit all 50 American states

Did you know? In 2008 Stephen Fry travelled across each of the 50 states of America in a London taxi. This incredible adventure provided an insight into the huge diversity of people, cultures, languages, beliefs and landscapes that have forged such a remarkable country.

- Celebrate the 'Day of the Dead' public holiday in Mexico
- Go to the Cave of Swallows

Did you know? The Cave of Swallows in Mexico, popular for vertical caving and B.A.S.E. jumping, is the largest known cave shaft in the world. New York's Chrysler building could fit in it easily.

- Go to Parícutin Volcano (widely considered one of the seven wonders of the natural world)
- See the Mayan ruins of Chichen Itza
- Visit Guatemala's Tikal National Park
- Climb Pacaya, an active volcano in Guatemala
- Attend the festival of Las Bolas de Fuego (Fire Balls) in El Salvador
- Visit Selvatura Park and take the canopy tour in the heart of Monteverde's cloud forest
- Enjoy a freshly rolled cigar in Cuba
- Ride the giant Dragon's Breath Zip Line in Haiti
- Kayak in the bioluminescent Bay of Fajardo in Puerto Rico
- Visit Necker Island (owned by Richard Branson and located in the British Virgin Islands)
- See Angel Falls in Venezuela
- Go to the Galápagos Islands
- Stand on the equator near Quito in Ecuador
- Hike Machu Picchu
- Go to Gocta Cataracts waterfalls and gorges in Peru
- Explore the Amazon rainforest

> Success story: In August 2010, Ed Stafford from Leicestershire became the first man to walk the 4,000-mile length of the Amazon River from the source to the Atlantic Ocean. This extraordinary journey, taking 859 days (about two and a half years) to complete, was steeped full of challenges and constant danger. Few people believed it even possible.

- Go to Salar de Uyuni in Bolivia (the world's largest salt flat)
- Hand glide over Rio de Janeiro, taking in the views of Christ the Redeemer
- Experience the Rio Carnival
- Go to the Fortaleza Canyon, Brazil
- Visit Iguazu Falls in Argentina
- Watch tango dancing in Buenos Aires

- Tour the Perito Moreno glacier in Argentina
- Stargaze in the Atacama Desert in Chile
- Swim in the largest swimming pool in the world, beside the sea in Chile
- See the statues of Easter Island

Worldwide

- Research the various Wonders of the World and go to all seven places from one of the lists (e.g. Seven Natural Wonders of the World, New7Wonders of the World)
- Live in another country for six months
- Visit 26 places each beginning with a different letter of the alphabet
- Go on a cruise
- Buy a round-the-world air ticket
- Fly first class
- Set foot on every continent in the world
- Swim in every ocean
- Spend your birthday in another country
- Celebrate New Year's Eve abroad
- Volunteer overseas for a month
- Go to the World's Fair

Did you know? The World's Fair is a large public exhibition held in various locations across the world. The majority of the structures built for this event are temporary, although the most famous exception is the Eiffel Tower, which was built for the 1889 World's Fair. Despite some critics at the time wanting it to be dismantled after the event it has become the most recognisable symbol of Paris.

- Go on a road trip
- Cross a country using only public transportation
- Try couch-surfing
- Enjoy a cheap and cheerful camping holiday
- Go glamping (glamorous camping)

- Do a golfing holiday
- Play a round of golf at a world-famous course
- Experience a day in a jungle
- Visit Antarctica
- Go polar bear watching in the Arctic
- Cross a glacier on foot
- See an active volcano
- Make a photo board of your favourite travel memories
- Put up a scratch map
- Mark on a map of the world all the places where you've been, add a photo from each place you've visited and pinpoint where you want to go next
- Turn up at an airport with your bags packed and randomly pick a destination to go to
- Throw a dart in a map and travel to where it lands
- Visit a place because of its name (it could share the same name as you or have an unusual sounding name)
- Visit a place that has featured in a scene from a film
- Become a space tourist!

"Don't listen to what they say. Go see."

(Chinese Proverb)

Improving Your Mind

Use it or lose it.

Throughout your life you are constantly learning. As you mature and begin to interact with the wider world, your ability to learn becomes increasingly important, both in terms of who you are now and who you will become.

Realising the importance of learning allows you to enjoy its many benefits. These include having better informed opinions, more to talk about and expressing yourself more confidently. Learning is its own reward and seeing yourself making progress is a satisfying experience.

> "Never stop learning, because life never stops teaching."
>
> (Unknown)

A great thing about learning is that it's a cheap and convenient way of passing your time. We all find ourselves with various amounts of spare time, such as between appointments or waiting for a train. Incorporating learning into your routine allows you to transform what you once perceived as dead time into an opportunity to memorise information or further your understanding of something. Today you can download a podcast or audiobook on almost any subject, access its contents within seconds and carry it with you at no inconvenience. A further benefit of the rise of electronic media is that second-hand books are readily available for very reasonable prices.

Just as a regular exercise regime can maintain your physical well-being, mental exercise leads to a healthy and responsive brain. Ways in which you can keep your brain in good working order include playing strategy games, doing word or number puzzles, reading, learning new things and having a varied number of different interests.

Today we have unprecedented access to information of all kinds at our fingertips and this brings many benefits. However, not taking the time to interrogate, understand and place this information into context could be putting our ability to learn in jeopardy. Our memory needs to be exercised regularly to stay in optimum condition.

Memory training

- Identify your learning style (you may be a visual, auditory or kinaesthetic learner)
- Research ways to improve your memory
- Practice a memory technique (e.g. rehearsal, first letter mnemonics, the method of loci)

Once you become familiar with different methods of memorising, you can apply them to remember faces, names, dates, telephone numbers and lists in your everyday life.

Did you know? Taxi drivers have to gain 'The Knowledge' in order to run a traditional black cab in London. This demanding training course results in an intimate familiarity with the streets within a six-mile radius of Charing Cross. Scientists at University College London carried out brain scans and discovered that taxi drivers have a larger hippocampus, the area of the brain associated with navigation, compared with other people. They also found that part of the hippocampus grew larger as they spent more time in their job, since they were repeatedly using this area of the brain to recall detailed mental maps and routes within the City.

Here are some ideas for your Birthday List of things you can learn:

Words & language

- How to say '*I love you*' in seven different languages
- A poem

- A new word every week
- Twenty-six new words from the dictionary, each starting with a different letter of the alphabet
- The Greek alphabet
- The phonetic alphabet
- Words that define popular phobias (e.g. aerophobia is the fear of flying, coulrophobia is the fear of clowns)
- Words that describe various collectors (e.g. a philatelist collects stamps, a bibliophile collects books)
- The collective nouns for groups of animals, birds and insects (e.g. a parliament of owls, a prickle of porcupines)
- Names of various species of baby animals (e.g. a baby hare is a leveret, a baby goose is a gosling)
- Definitions for sciences and studies (e.g. vexillology is the study of flags, selenology is the study of the moon)

Sport

- Boxing weights
- The offside rule in football
- Laws or rules of a sport
- Wimbledon champions
- Snooker world champions
- Football World Cup winners
- Super Bowl champions
- Formula 1 winners
- Tour de France winners
- Grand National winners
- Host cities of the modern Olympic Games

History

- All British prime ministers
- American presidents
- Kings and queens of Britain

- The six wives of Henry VIII
- The timeline of the major wars, famous civilisations and empires
- Battles of the American Civil War
- A famous person who influenced or changed the world
- Every *Time* Person of the Year since 1927 (the individual, group, idea or object, that, for better or for worse, has most influenced world events during the year)
- Significant historical events (e.g. the Great Fire of London in 1666, the Great Train Robbery of 1963)
- Native American tribes and their famous leaders
- The most famous ships in history

World and ancient religions

- All the religious holidays and festivals and what they mean (e.g. Diwali, commonly known as the 'Festival of Lights')
- Hindu gods and goddesses
- The Four Noble Truths and the Noble Eightfold Path of Buddhism
- Five Pillars of Islam
- Prohibitions in Sikhism
- The five Ks worn by Sikhs
- Biblical Jewish leaders and prophets
- Jewish rituals and ritual objects
- The Ten Commandments
- Names of the twelve disciples of Jesus
- The Lord's Prayer
- Famous popes in history

> Did you know? Nicholas Breakspear, born in Hertfordshire, was the one and only English Pope.

- Gods and goddesses in Roman or Greek mythology
- The twelve labours of Hercules
- Norse gods and goddesses

- The Wonders of the World
- Bones of the human body
- The seven chakras
- Parts of a flower
- Different cloud types
- Why the sky is blue
- Charles Darwin's theory of evolution
- Different types of fish
- Names of bird species
- Types of butterflies found in the British Isles
- The dinosaurs that once inhabited our planet
- Inventors whose ideas led to significant scientific breakthroughs
- Various types of bridge structure (e.g. beam, cantilever, suspension)

Did you know? In 1968, London Bridge became the largest antique ever sold. The five-arched stone bridge was bought by an American businessman for $2,460,000. It was shipped out stone by stone and reassembled in Lake Havasu City, Arizona.

- Nobel Prize winners
- The famous equation $E=mc^2$ and what it means
- The periodic table

A must hear! Listen to 'The Elements', a song by Tom Lehrer which recites the names of all the chemical elements known at the time of writing, up to number 102 (learning this song for yourself could even be an item on your Birthday List...)

- The geological timescale of the earth

- Structure of the earth
- Constellations in the night sky
- The order of planets from the sun, using first letter mnemonics

Did you know? All pictures of the solar system that we see in textbooks are not drawn to scale. They are necessarily deceitful in order to get all the planets onto the same piece of paper. In Bill Bryson's book, *A Short History of Nearly Everything*, he explains how Neptune, in reality, is five times farther from Jupiter than Jupiter is from us. If the solar system was drawn to scale, with Earth reduced to the size of a pea, Jupiter would be over 300 metres away and Pluto (which has now been downgraded to a dwarf planet) would be two and a half kilometres away (and about the size of a bacterium, so you wouldn't be able to see it anyway).

- History of space exploration
- Names of the first ten men to walk on the moon

Geography

- Where countries are in the world
- Capital cities of the world
- All the countries in Europe
- What the largest or smallest countries are in the world by size or population
- Flags of the world
- Currencies of the world
- Member countries of the Commonwealth
- The 50 states in the USA and their state capitals
- All the counties in the UK
- The inhabited islands that are part of the British Isles
- The ten largest deserts, rivers, lakes or seas on Earth

- The common instruments that make up an orchestra
- Popular Italian musical terms
- The male and female ranges of singing voices
- Every verse of your national anthem
- Roman numerals
- Names of shapes and how many sides they have
- Why the days of the week and the months of the year are named as they are
- The traditional anniversary gifts for each year of marriage
- The names of people who appear on modern banknotes
- How to convert metric to imperial measurements
- Measurement terms, together with what they measure and who they were named after (e.g. the Beaufort scale measures wind speed and was named after Sir Francis Beaufort)
- The signs of the zodiac
- Car badges
- The 13 times table
- The formula for velocity
- How to calculate probability
- All the 168 prime numbers under 1,000
- How to calculate the area of a circle
- Ranks in the military
- Champagne bottle sizes
- Patron saints (e.g. Saint Sebastian is the patron saint of athletes)
- The works of William Shakespeare in chronological order
- All the Bond films and the name of each actor who played the lead role

Did you know? In the James Bond books, 007 drinks whisky far more often than the famous vodka Martini, shaken not stirred.

- Best Picture, Best Actor and Best Actress Oscar winners
- Real names of celebrities who go by stage names

Did you know? Cary Grant's real name was Archibald Leach, which was the same name as the character played by John Cleese in the film, *A Fish Called Wanda*. Cleese, who co-wrote the film with Charles Crichton, said it was the closest he would ever get to actually being Cary Grant.

Cultivating Interests

Try something new.

Your happiness increases when you're doing things you love. Having an interest is a beautiful thing. When you have some spare time it's there waiting for you, allowing you the opportunity to indulge in something that makes you happy.

Experiencing new things allows you to learn more about who you are. The more you try, the more you do, and the more you do, the more you know. We all have different aspirations and abilities that make us unique; trying new things is the best route to finding your true passion.

"If you never try, you'll never know what you are capable of."

(John Barrow)

Being interested makes you interesting, as genuine interest in another person's thoughts and opinions demonstrates you are a good listener and builds a connection. The more diverse your range of experiences, the more rounded and balanced your outlook. Therefore, more experience of anything means a better understanding of everything.

Nobody is born with a natural ability to effortlessly create incredible things. Masterpieces, such as the Sistine Chapel in the Vatican City, are often the result of unbelievable amounts of hard work and dedication.

"If you knew how much work went into it, you would not call it genius."

(Michelangelo)

Neurologist Daniel Levitin wrote, *'ten thousand hours of practice is required to achieve the level of mastery associated with being a world-class expert – in anything.'* Bill Gates, Mozart and The Beatles have all put in well over 10,000 hours of practice each within their respective professions. To be the best of the best, it doesn't just boil down to opportunity and a natural talent. Anyone can achieve great things with the power of belief, hard work and dedication.

"Nothing is impossible. The word itself says, 'I'm possible'!"

(Audrey Hepburn)

Did you know? Gardening tasks, such as pushing a lawn mower, raking leaves, digging holes and pulling weeds, use muscle groups all over the body, providing you with a good, calorie-burning workout. Furthermore, gardens are increasingly being recognised as a way to improve the health of care home residents, specifically people with dementia. It is a stress-relieving, mood-improving activity that can be done on any scale. Even if you don't have a garden, you could still invest in a pot or window box and feel the benefits as your seeds grow.

- Plant a herb garden
- Establish your own vegetable patch
- Start a compost heap
- Make your own wormery
- Grow a sunflower (have a competition as to who can grow the tallest)

Did you know? Nurturing another living thing can have a hugely beneficial effect on your life. In the 1970s, Judith Rodin and Ellen Langer conducted an experiment with nursing home residents. One group of elderly people had the freedom to make choices and the responsibility of caring for a plant. A second group were given no instructions to make their own decisions. They were also given houseplants, but were told that the nursing staff would care for them. After a year and a half, the researchers found that the first group of people were happier, healthier and living longer.

- Grow a cactus
- Identify the names of all the flowers in your garden
- Create a hanging basket

> Did you know? Bees pollinate 70 out of the top 100 human food crops that feed 90% of the world. Without bees, many plants would die off and half the amount of fruit and vegetables would be available to us.

- Plant flowers in your garden that will attract honeybees
- Enter a local gardening competition
- Plant a tree

"The best time to plant a tree was 20 years ago. The second best time is now."

(Chinese Proverb)

- Landscape your garden
- Start a bonsai collection
- Decorate a tree with lanterns, ribbons or wind chimes
- Look at the night sky through a telescope
- Go mudlarking
- Become a PADI certified scuba diver
- Join a sailing club and participate in a regatta
- Participate in geocaching (and plant your own geocache!)

> Did you know? Special containers called geocaches are hidden all over the world waiting for you to find them. You just need the app on your mobile and a GPS signal to locate one. There may be one right by you now!

- Milk a cow
- Shear a sheep
- Rear chickens
- Use a lasso

- Handle a bird of prey
- Go strawberry picking
- Crush grapes with your bare feet (to make wine)
- Find your way to the centre of a maze
- Take your dog to agility training sessions and enter a competition
- Experience three different types of fishing
- Go rockpooling
- Visit a top birdwatching hotspot
- Book a horse riding lesson
- Drive a rage buggy
- Drive a tractor
- Go clay pigeon shooting
- Hit the bullseye of an archery target
- Play a basket of golf balls on the driving range

Take an interest

- Increase your knowledge of what is happening in the world by downloading a news app
- Vote in an election
- Write a letter to your MP with a useful suggestion or request
- Start or support a movement on a cause you passionately believe in
- Watch Martin Luther King Jr's *'I Have a Dream'* speech

"*Your life does not get better by chance, it gets better by change.*"

(Jim Rohn)

- Get involved with your neighbourhood or local community
- Become a member of the National Trust
- Obtain an English Heritage membership
- Witness the launch of a space shuttle
- View a documentary about a topic you know very little about
- Watch an online TED Talk on a topic of your choosing

- Learn how to use DJ equipment to mix
- Research your family history and draw up your family tree
- Trace the history of your home
- Get a pet
- Start a collection of something that you have a passion for
- Research the history of your favourite interest or hobby
- Join a local church bell ringing society (become a campanologist)
- Learn how to play a new game
- Solve a tricky maths problem

- Learn to speak a foreign language
- Enrol on a sign language course
- Learn to read Braille
- Attend a lip reading course
- Learn how to solve cryptic crosswords
- Write your name in Egyptian hieroglyphs
- Study etymology (the history of words and their origins)

- Broaden your knowledge about major events in history (e.g. World Wars I and II, the Renaissance)
- Join a historical re-enactment society
- Be part of an archaeological dig
- Join an amateur theatre group
- Take part in a cosplay event
- Become part of a ghost hunting team
- Buy a calligraphy set (write your next Birthday List with it...)
- Make a huge structure out of Lego

Did you know? In September 2009, television presenter James May and 1,000 helpers built the world's first full-size Lego house. Consisting of 3.3 million Lego bricks, the two-storey house was even equipped with a working toilet and hot shower.

- Take a photo of one of your favourite places in all four seasons
- Complete the 365-day photo challenge by taking a picture every day for a year
- Attend an astrophotography lesson
- Get started on Photoshop
- Use a Raspberry Pi to learn about computer programming
- Create your own website
- Design a phone app
- Post a YouTube video
- Decipher your dreams using a guide book

Tip: Keep a notebook by your bed and write down your dreams immediately to help you remember them.

- Learn the art of tasseography (tea leaf reading)
- Study the basics of palmistry

- Learn how to interpret tarot cards and perform a reading for someone
- Complete a flair bartending course
- Be an extra in a film
- Form a band
- Embark on singing lessons
- Join a local singing group (e.g. a gospel style choir, an a cappella group)
- Learn how to read music
- Perfect a new song on a musical instrument
- Start taking music lessons

Did you know? Playing a musical instrument has many long-term benefits, including sharpened concentration, better memory, improved patience, increased productivity and more confidence.

"Playing music is the brain's equivalent of a full body workout."

(Anita Collins)

- Finish a Sudoku book
- Complete a touch typing course
- Make yourself an item of clothing
- Participate in the Red Bull Soapbox Race
- Exhibit your art in a gallery
- Learn how to create a different hairstyle (e.g. a fishtail plait, victory rolls)
- Perfect a new make-up technique
- Experiment with nail art for special occasions
- Try henna hand painting
- Learn hand or foot reflexology
- Enrol on a massage course
- Research the basics of crystal healing

- Take an aromatherapy course
- Learn the basics of ikebana (the Japanese art of flower arranging)
- Design your own house
- Read up on the fundamentals of feng shui
- Declutter and tidy your entire home

A must read! *'The Life-Changing Magic of Tidying'* by Marie Kondo provides an inspirational step-by-step method to help you clear and tidy your home.

Skillful accomplishments

- Escape from handcuffs or a straitjacket
- Choreograph a dance to a song
- Learn how to twerk
- Perform a burlesque routine
- Enter a talent contest
- Perform on stage
- Throw a boomerang so that it returns to you
- Learn 'The Cup Song' routine (performed by Anna Kendrick in the film *'Pitch Perfect'*)
- Master the lyrics of a challenging song or rap (e.g. 'Gangnam Style' by PSY)

Did you know? Rap stands for 'rhythm and poetry'.

- Whip a tablecloth out from underneath a laid table without disturbing any items
- Pick up a piece of paper from the floor using your teeth (only your feet can touch the floor)
- Walk over hot coals (aided by expert supervision)
- Attempt tightrope walking

- Master the art of ventriloquy
- Set a Guinness World Record
- Design and build a robot
- Learn to write with your opposite hand

- Perfectly tie a bow tie
- Try out different knots on a necktie
- Perfect a figure skating move
- Learn to do a hockey stop on rollerblades
- Perform a wheelie on a bike
- Learn how to do an 'ollie' on a skateboard
- Perfect a trick shot in pool
- Learn a magic trick

"Challenges are what make life interesting and overcoming them is what makes life meaningful."

(Joshua J. Marine)

- Master juggling with four balls
- Perform a Zippo lighter trick
- Light a match with one hand
- Learn a pen-spinning routine
- Achieve a turkey in tenpin bowling (three consecutive strikes)
- Learn how to solve a Rubik's Cube
- Successfully see a magic eye picture
- Score 180 with three darts
- Master a yo-yo trick
- Learn how to shuffle a deck of cards in three different ways

Extreme sports are all about exhilaration, experience and danger. If you enjoy adventure, pushing your physical capabilities and challenging your fears, extreme activities may well be for you. A good way to get started is to join a club where you will be able to access expert advice and equipment. You will need skills, nerve and dedication.

- Take up a new boardsport
- Experience a new motorsport
- Try a new watersport
- Experience a mountaineering activity
- Challenge yourself with a free fall or flying activity

A must watch! 'People Are Awesome' is an inspiring montage of people displaying spectacular stunts (available to watch on YouTube).

"There is nothing you cannot achieve. No skill you cannot master. We're all flesh, and bone, and guts. We're just people. Nothing is out of our reach. Nothing is impossible. People can do anything. Because...PEOPLE ARE AWESOME."

('People are Awesome' channel trailer narration)

Art

- Knit something
- Finish a colouring book
- Complete a 'paint by numbers'
- Create a finger painting
- Make Chinese wishing stars
- Quilt a cushion
- Create a picture using pressed flowers
- Use quilling to create a picture
- Make a collage
- Create marbled paper
- Produce your own rubber stamped art rocks
- Make a bar of soap or bath bomb
- Decorate an egg

"Every artist was first an amateur."

(Ralph Emerson)

- Paint a design on a mug, plate or vase
- Create a piece of art using pyrography
- Learn to emboss or deboss a design onto paper
- Attend a glassblowing class
- Make a candle
- Produce a rainbow rose
- Design your own kite
- Create a mosaic
- Model a balloon animal
- Make a puppet
- Construct a scarecrow
- Transform a bookcase into a doll's house
- Design and print your own T-shirt
- Weave a rug or basket
- Decorate something using découpage
- Produce a collagraph

- Create a pattern using string art
- Design and make a miniature village
- Make something using papier-mâché
- Create a coaster using a beadwork technique
- Design and make an item of jewellery
- Make a loom band
- Crochet a scarf
- Make a hacky sack
- Master an origami piece
- Fold a napkin into a rose
- Create a peg doll
- Carve an ice sculpture
- Build a sand sculpture
- Sculpt a clay vase using a potter's wheel
- Make a ship in a bottle
- Build a model aeroplane
- Invent a board game
- Create a scrapbook
- Research creative and beautiful ways to wrap presents (every time you give a gift make it look really special)
- Make your own Christmas wreath, tree or table decorations
- Decorate an Easter tree

Literature

Here are some ideas for your Birthday List of things you could read:

- One book every month
- Five books from the Modern Library's '100 Best Novels' list
- A Nobel Prize winner's book
- A book from the banned books list
- Your friend's favourite book of all time
- All the books ever written by your favourite author
- A broadsheet newspaper, cover to cover
- A book of religious teachings (e.g. the *Bhagavad Gita*, the Bible)

> Did you know? **The shortest verse in the King James Version of the Bible is John 11:35 which contains only two words,** *'Jesus wept'.*

Here are some ideas for your Birthday List of things you could write:

- A letter to yourself to open in ten years
- A blog
- A diary or journal
- Your own life story
- A song
- A poem
- A univocalic (a piece of writing using just one vowel)
- Your own comedy sketch
- A film script
- A book

> Success story: **George Orwell wrote** *'Animal Farm'* **in just three months. As a result of the publication of this book in 1945, Orwell became perhaps one of the most important and influential British novelists of the day.**

- Start a book club
- Join a literature or creative writing group
- Participate in NaNoWriMo (National Novel Writing Month) in November

"A writer who waits for ideal conditions under which to work will die without putting a word on paper."

(E.B. White)

Practical skills

- Perform an oil change on your car
- Learn how to change a car tyre
- Assemble an emergency kit to keep in the boot of your car
- Start a fire without a lighter or matches
- Learn how to make your own compass
- Make your own catapult
- Attend a woodcarving workshop
- Build a birdhouse
- Make your own spice rack
- Construct a bookcase
- Completely redecorate a room in your home
- Learn upholstery
- Refurbish an old piece of furniture
- Build a treehouse
- Make an igloo
- Restore a classic car
- Build your own kit car
- Learn how to tie three different types of knot
- Cook on a camping stove
- Go on a survival weekend
- Receive CPR training
- Learn how to perform the Heimlich manoeuvre

Entertainment & cultural experiences

- Watch the top 250 films on the Internet Movie Database
- See every film that has ever won a Best Picture Oscar
- Watch every film starring your favourite actor or actress
- Catch a film at a drive-in or open air cinema
- Visit a film festival
- Be a member of the audience in a TV show
- Camp at a music festival
- Get tickets to watch your favourite band or singer
- See a musical

- Go to a live stand-up comedy performance
- Watch a Shakespeare play
- Go to the opera
- Watch a ballet
- Visit the circus
- Watch a pantomime
- Attend a fashion show
- Go to a masquerade ball
- See five famous paintings or sculptures
- Visit a museum
- Attend a classic car show
- Watch a drag race
- Go to a monster trucks event
- Experience a major sporting event
- Attend a steam rally
- Go on a ghost walk
- Take part in a tea dance
- Go to a village fete
- Attend a May Day celebration
- Go to a 'Burns Night' celebration at the end of January
- Attend a scarecrow festival
- Visit a 'Kitty Café'
- Go to a greyhound or horse racing track
- Visit your local bingo hall
- Go to a casino
- Take part in an organised treasure hunt
- Visit the birthplace or a gravesite of a cultural icon
- Go to church on Christmas Eve to celebrate Midnight Mass
- Step barefoot in a mosque
- Visit a monastery
- Walk inside a pagoda

Money And Work Life

To be wealthy is a state of mind.

Money surrounds us in modern life, making its presence constantly felt. Whether we like it or not, our society has put a pound sign on everything from drinking water to parking a car. It's all too easy to let your perception of money become negative by feeling that you don't have enough of it.

"To be without some of the things you want is an indispensable part of happiness."

(Bertrand Russell)

There is no need to get bogged down by the pursuit of riches. Once our basic needs have been met, money contributes very little to our overall happiness and well-being. However, we must acknowledge that both money and work life are limiting factors upon each of us and our Birthday Lists.

By taking care of finances and controlling spending, you can become empowered to make changes in life when required. Cultivating a mentality aimed at saving as much money as possible increases your ability to do the things you want, when you want.

> *"You aren't wealthy until you have something money can't buy."*
>
> (Garth Brooks)

Things that give us meaning and purpose in our lives bring us greater happiness than more superficial things like wealth and status. You may be able to craft your job in ways that help you find meaning at work. This isn't about changing core responsibilities, it is about your approach to carrying out your duties. Most jobs allow for this in some way, from entry level to senior management. Taking pride in your work and being fully involved in your job will enhance not only your happiness, but also the happiness of those around you in the workplace.

Pursuing a vocation doesn't necessarily need to involve a career or a job. It can be obtained by following a passion or dream, which may not always involve paid work. Some people realise their vocation through the pursuit of certain interests or activities, volunteer or service work. A great example of someone who discovered their calling in life is Mahatma Gandhi, who followed his heart by turning his back on a lucrative career as a lawyer in order to fulfil his vocation of leading the people of India to independence and self-governance.

> *"Choose a job you love, and you will never have to work a day in your life."*
>
> (Confucius)

This book is not designed to help you rapidly progress in your career or earn enormous amounts of money. You might choose something from this section for your Birthday List if you feel you want a new challenge, or something that will encourage you to make better decisions about your finances.

Many people think that if they become successful then they will be happy. However, recent discoveries have found that the reverse is true: **Happiness leads to success.** When we are feeling good and positive our brains are more engaged, creative, motivated, energetic, resilient, and productive.

Making money

*"It's no trick to make a lot of money...
If what you want to do is make a lot of
money."*

(Citizen Kane, 1941 film)

- Buy something and sell it for a profit
- Sell an item on the Internet
- Do a car boot sale
- Auction something off
- Learn about stocks and shares and make an investment in the stock market
- Use crowdfunding to raise money for a project

> Did you know? In 1987, Mike Hayes of Illinois convinced 2.8 million people to send him a penny each to pay for all four years of his college education. He graduated in 1991 with a degree in food science and no student loan. Hayes said there was a thousand dollars left over after all his college expenses were paid, so he gave it to a student from one of the families that sent him money. At the end of it all, Mike said, *'I just want to express my thanks to everyone...right now I'm feeling that the world is a pretty great place.'*

- Read a bestselling book about getting rich
- Ask your employer for a pay rise
- Learn how to make money from a blog or webpage
- Enter a competition once a month
- Start a 'cottage industry'
- Get a second job
- Take in a lodger or a foreign exchange student
- Rent out your driveway, garage or parking space
- Invest in property

Saving money

- Go to a garage sale
- Buy items from second-hand stores
- Start a trust fund or savings account for a child
- Put money aside into a savings account every month
- Join your company's sharesave scheme
- Pay off your credit card
- Switch banks (if a better deal can be found elsewhere)
- Check your credit rating
- Go for a month without buying anything that isn't a necessity

> Tip: Print off a calendar for the month and use it to record how much you spend each day. It can really help you to stay focused and you may be surprised at how rewarding it is to write a big '£0' on all the days when you spend no money.

- Borrow books for free from a local library
- Permanently swap ten products that you buy on a regular basis for cheaper 'own brand' alternatives
- Subscribe online to receive free cosmetic and make-up samples
- Shop at a cheaper supermarket and see how much you save
- Look into cheaper service providers to reduce energy bills
- Check your mortgage deal

- Create a weekly spending budget
- Set up a joint account to manage your bills more effectively
- Pay money into your pension
- Redeem all your loyalty card points
- Go through your kitchen cupboards monthly to keep on top of what you have
- Make a packed lunch for work every day
- Prepare a dish once a month that can be frozen in portions
- Plan your menu for the week ahead

Personal development in the workplace

- Research your personality type to find what kind of job you might enjoy
- Seek careers guidance
- Write or update your CV
- Research how to be successful in job interviews
- Secure some work experience to gain insight into a job that appeals to you
- Attain a driving licence
- Research ways to be a success at work
- Find a mentor who can advise you on career development
- Ask your employer to sponsor you to do something that you want to do
- Become a first aider or appointed fire warden
- Attend an inspirational seminar
- Enrol on a professional development course
- Attend a business etiquette course
- Read up on tips to improve your body language and put them into practice
- Attend a public speaking course
- Deliver a speech or presentation to a large audience
- Get a degree
- Complete an NLP training course
- Become a mentor
- Apply for a promotion
- Get a new job (perhaps research the top 100 employers)

- Start your own business
- Give thought to your job or career: What do YOU want to do?

There are thousands upon thousands of job titles in the world. With so many options, it's perfectly normal to feel confused when looking for a new job or deciding upon your next career move. Overcoming the fear of change, especially in tough economic times, is a key factor in changing jobs. It's not uncommon for people to feel so anxious about making the wrong choice that they end up making no choice at all and stay in jobs that do not make them happy. Changing jobs might be the best decision of your life.

> Did you know? Bill Gates dropped out of Harvard University in 1975. He went on to become the world's richest man.

> Success story: Levi Roots appeared on *Dragons' Den* in 2007 and convinced Peter Jones and Richard Farleigh to invest £50,000 in his Jamaican jerk spice product, Reggae Reggae Sauce, in return for 40% of his company. When it first went on sale, Sainsbury's had expected the sauce to sell 50,000 bottles in its first year. In fact, it sold 40,000–50,000 bottles per week! Roots continued to grow the company and in 2014 he had an estimated net worth of £35million.

Other people aren't always right, so don't let them tell you that you can't do something. The vast majority of people encounter knockbacks and challenges before they get to where they want to be. Clint Eastwood was fired from Universal in 1959 by a studio executive who told him he spoke too slowly and his Adam's apple stuck out too far. Elvis Presley's music teacher, at L.C. Humes High School in Memphis, gave him a 'C' and told him he couldn't sing. You haven't failed unless you give up.

"You may have to fight a battle more than once to win it."

(Margaret Thatcher)

Workplace culture

Finding a job within an organisation that has a great culture will have a
remarkably positive impact on your life. Research indicates that happiness
in the workplace means greater productivity, greater profit margin, lower
staff turnover and fewer sick days. You can contribute towards creating
a great culture within the workplace by doing little things that go a long
way. Positive behaviour encourages positive behaviour.

*"Act as if what you do makes a difference.
It does."*

(William James)

- Coordinate a team building day out with your colleagues
- Arrange a sweepstake for a national event that is coming up
- Organise a fundraising event
- Compile a list of work birthdays and set up a system to make sure everyone gets a card
- Decorate your colleague's desk when it's their birthday
- Establish 'Fact Fridays' where you each find an interesting fact to share
- Start an office tradition
- Create a mini league Fantasy Football Dream Team
- Start a cake rota

Work-life balance

- Turn off your work mobile phone as soon as you leave work every day
- Go for a walk on your lunch break at least once a week
- Hire a personal coach who can tell you what you can do to achieve optimal balance
- Take a time management course
- Create a timetable to record your commitments and identify your free time

"No one ever said on their deathbed, 'I wish I'd spent more time at the office'."

(Rabbi Harold Kushner)

If you've ever thought that you do not have enough hours in the day, Benjamin Franklin and his life achievements will make your head spin. Franklin, who was one of seventeen children, was a polymath, a leading author, printer, political theorist, politician, postmaster, scientist, musician, inventor, satirist, civic activist, statesman and a diplomat.

Despite his numerous professions and keen interests, Franklin was neither a workaholic nor an insomniac. He followed a simple daily schedule that was split into six time periods:

5 a.m. until 8 a.m.:	Get up, wash, breakfast, personal study and preparation for work
8 a.m. until 12 p.m.:	Work
12 p.m. until 2 p.m.:	Read or overlook accounts and lunch
2 p.m. until 6 p.m.:	Work
6 p.m. until 10 p.m.:	Dinner, wrapping up the day and personal time
10 p.m. until 5 a.m.:	Sleep

By using this simple yet well thought out time management system, Franklin invented the lightning rod (he was awarded the Copley medal for his work in electricity), swim fins, bifocals, the Franklin stove, a carriage odometer, the long arm, the glass harmonica and many other things.

Franklin was the first scientist to study and map the Gulf Stream. He established one of the first volunteer firefighting companies and the first fire insurance company. He helped launch projects to pave, clean and light Philadelphia's streets. He started the Library Company, the University of Pennsylvania, the American Philosophical Society, the Pennsylvania Hospital and the Franklin and Marshall College. He was a member of the learned societies of many nations and received several honorary degrees, including a doctorate from St Andrews.

In 1776, Franklin signed the *Declaration of Independence* and one of his last public acts was writing an anti-slavery treatise in 1789. Franklin died in 1790, aged 84, and 20,000 people attended his funeral.

Just Because You Can

Do it now. Regret it never.

'Just because you can' is the main reason for placing any item onto your Birthday List. This section mostly focuses on easy, affordable, enjoyable experiences that you should be able to tick off relatively quickly to get your list underway.

There may be certain things on your list that can only be accomplished under specific conditions. Make sure you don't hesitate to do them when the opportunities spring up. If it is windy, seize the day and go fly your kite!

> "Realise deeply that the present moment is all you ever have."

(*The Power of Now* by Eckhart Tolle)

Shaking up your routine is good for your brain. Routines do not provide the brain with stimulation. They are run by our subconscious and use very little brain energy. Benedict Carey, author of the book, *How We Learn*, says our routines limit our brain's ability to build skills and knowledge. Placing yourself in unfamiliar places, trying new things and changing your daily movements can maximise the brain's effectiveness, allowing you to be more creative, productive and successful.

Make the most of your life and take every opportunity that arises. Say 'yes' as much as possible and don't let the door close on a chance for good times and happy memories.

- Lie on the grass making cloud animals
- Make a daisy chain
- Find a four-leaf clover
- Rollerblade down your street
- Fly a kite
- Ride a unicycle
- Walk on stilts
- Use a pogo stick
- Get a Slinky to make its way down the stairs
- Use a rope swing to jump into a river or a lake
- Make your own rope swing in the woods

"Growing old is mandatory. Growing up is optional."

(Carroll Bryant)

- Build a house of cards
- Make a snow angel
- Create something out of snow (be creative!)
- Have a water pistol, pillow or snowball fight
- Go sledging
- Hold a paper aeroplane competition
- Go puddle jumping in the rain
- Play a game of laser tag
- Create a fight scene using lightsabers
- Make a den
- Build a giant sandcastle
- Learn to whistle or wolf whistle

- Perfect a difficult tongue twister (e.g. 'The sixth sick sheik's sixth sheep's sick')
- Sock slide across the floor
- Feed the ducks
- Make your voice echo underneath a bridge
- Climb a tree
- Go conker picking
- Engineer an April Fool's Day trick
- Create your own puppet show
- Inhale helium and talk funny
- Eat a sugar-coated doughnut without licking your lips
- Run down an escalator the wrong way
- Skim stones in a lake or sea
- Do something that you were never allowed to do as a child

Beautiful life experiences

- Wish on a shooting star
- Experience a solar or lunar eclipse
- Watch the sun rise or set over the ocean
- See the sun rise and the sun set in the same day
- Witness a meteor shower
- Release an eco-friendly Chinese lantern
- Tell someone that you love them
- Kiss under the mistletoe
- Share a kiss in the rain
- Take a walk in the rain
- Hold a newborn baby
- Bottle-feed a lamb
- Shower in a waterfall
- Sleep in a hammock
- Dive off a boat into the sea
- Dance barefoot in the rain
- Go for a moonlit walk on a beach
- Swim in the moonlight
- Sleep under the stars

- Take a cold shower
- Go skinny-dipping
- Play strip poker
- Spend the whole day naked
- Pose as a life model for an art class
- Go to a nudist beach
- Stay in a fully furnished treehouse
- Spend a night in a haunted house
- Stay in a castle
- Identify a bad habit that you have and attempt to break it
- Do something that absolutely terrifies you
- Hold a tarantula
- Put a python on your shoulders
- Swim with wild dolphins
- Fly in a stunt plane
- Sit in the cockpit of a Concorde
- Take a submarine tour
- Test drive your dream car
- Drive around a world-famous race circuit
- Go on a Ferris wheel
- Ride the top five most extreme rollercoasters in the world
- Crowd-surf
- Sing karaoke
- Bury a time capsule
- Recreate a famous album cover
- Re-enact a famous movie scene
- Have a photograph taken of you 'planking'
- Create a new voicemail greeting
- Don't use your car for a whole month
- Go technology-free for one week
- See the iconic Coca-Cola truck on its Christmas tour
- Fry an egg on the pavement on a scorching hot day
- Ride a mechanical rodeo bull
- Take a Segway PT tour

- Walk to the top of a lighthouse
- Have a ride on a snowmobile
- Drive a husky sled
- Try Zorbing
- Experience wave running
- Ride on a banana boat
- Go parasailing
- Ride on the world's largest waterslide
- Experience zero gravity (or weightlessness)

> A must hear! Listen to the song 'Everybody's Free (To Wear Sunscreen)' by Baz Luhrmann.

- Book a make-up lesson
- Visit a professional for a colour analysis to discover which colours make the best of your complexion
- Attend a lesson on dressing for your body shape
- Get a body piercing
- Design your own tattoo
- Dye or chalk your hair
- Get a new haircut
- Grow a beard and leave it for a month
- Have your portrait painted
- Take a vow of silence for a day
- Have a past life reading
- Be hypnotised
- Attend a traditional séance
- Use a Ouija board
- Calculate your carbon footprint and implement changes to reduce it:
    - Cycle or walk to work
    - Car share with a colleague who lives close by
    - Buy only free range eggs/organic meat
    - Buy local produce
    - Go vegetarian on weekdays

- Invest in a 'bag for life'
- Recycle glass, paper, plastics and food waste
- Use eco-friendly cleaning products
- Invest in energy efficient appliances
- Where possible, change all bulbs in your house to low energy light bulbs
- Insulate your house
- Install solar panels

Did you know? To prevent single use plastic water bottles from being consumed, musician Jack Johnson requests that filtered water dispensing stations are available at his concerts. This allows his fans to refill their water bottles and also save money.

- Complete *The Legend of Zelda: Ocarina of Time* (widely considered to be the greatest video game ever made)
- Apply to take part in a TV game show
- Celebrate an unusual national day of the year (e.g. Hat Day on 15 January, The Most Wuthering Heights Day Ever on 16 July)
- Say *'yes'* to everything for a whole day

A must read or watch! *Yes Man* by Danny Wallace is a light-hearted, feel-good book written about his real-life experiences when he challenges himself to say *'yes'* to all invitations and opportunities that come his way. This book became a hugely successful film (12A rated) starring Jim Carrey in the lead role.

- Send a message in a bottle
- Tie a note to a balloon and let it go
- Leave an inspirational note inside a book for someone to find

- Display your favourite quote on a wall in your home
- Have a complaint-free day

> **Did you know?** Complaining tends to divert your attention to the bad parts of your life, rather than the good parts. By not complaining, it will help you to focus more on the positives.

- Remind yourself of ten things every day that you are grateful for
- Write down your biggest regret in life. Now do something about it (live a life of no regrets)
- Create a vision board displaying images of your hopes and dreams

> **True story:** A close friend was feeling sad after breaking up with her partner, and had some money worries. One night she drew a picture of a house with a rainbow and a happy couple in the garden. This was the life that she wanted for herself. Her friend visited her in the morning and took the picture home to save it from being thrown away. A couple of years later, the friend who had drawn the picture announced that she was getting married and had recently moved in with her fiancé. On her birthday she was given her picture back on a card...her vision had come true.

> **A must read or watch!** *The Secret,* by Rhonda Byrne. By applying the powerful knowledge of *The Secret* to your life you will get the life that you want, including health, wealth, success, love and happiness. It can transform your life.

This Time Next Year

Live the life you love.

Now it's time to write your Birthday List!

This book can't contain everything that you might want to do. The possibilities are endless, with new crazes to participate in and ever-evolving technology to sample year-on-year. That said, this book and the philosophy behind it can be used not just for this year, but for the rest of your life.

Ultimately, the inspiration behind your Birthday List has to come from you. It must, or it just won't work. This book covers a selection of general areas where you might find inspiration, but it's your Birthday List and everything that you put on it is totally up to you.

You're more likely to do things you've said out loud and even more likely to do things that you've written down. So talk to your friends and family, and share your goals and ideas with them. You'll be motivated by engaging with other positive people, plus you might just find someone that wants to make wonderful memories with you!

"Happiness is not a goal...it's a by-product of a life well lived."

(Eleanor Roosevelt)

Take some time to reflect on something you've always said you wanted to do but, so far, never have. If it's still relevant and appropriate for this year then **put it on your Birthday List**!

Become an intentional creator of your life. Amazing things can be achieved with the belief that anything is possible. Know that people who achieve their goals do so with planning, passion, persistence and self-belief.

"Don't wait until everything is just right. It will never be perfect. There will always be challenges, obstacles and less than perfect conditions. So what. Get started now."

(Mark Victor Hansen)

Your actions can lead to life-changing achievements that will aid your personal growth, give an overwhelming sense of satisfaction and inspire other people. Spending more of your time engaged in positive activities that help you broaden your mind, learn new things and care for your body, will bring you happiness and help you to become the best possible version of yourself.

There's so much to be happy about and there are so many things out there waiting for you to explore and accomplish. It begins here with your Birthday List. So start putting things on your list and start what has the potential to be the best year of your life so far.

The Birthday List can make a difference both to your life and the lives of those around you. To what extent is completely up to you.

"Be the change that you wish to see in the world."

(Mahatma Gandhi)

Bibliography

BrainyQuote, 'Famous Quotes at BrainyQuote', https://www.brainyquote.com/

Goodreads.com, 'Popular Quotes', https://www.goodreads.com/quotes

Waters, Lea, University of Melbourne, 'Why Happiness is Contagious', World Economic Forum, 30 October 2015, https://www.weforum.org/agenda/2015/10/why-happiness-is-contagious/

Dolin, Ann, M.Ed, 'How Family Dinners Improve Students' Grades', Educational Connections Inc, http://ectutoring.com/resources/articles/family-dinners-improve-students-grades

Sharon M. Fruh, PhD, RN, FNP-BC, Jayne A. Fulkerson, PhD, Madhuri S. Mulekar, PhD, Lee Ann J. Kendrick, MEd, and Clista Clanton, MSLS, AHIP, 'The Surprising Benefits of the Family Meal', *The Journal for Nurse Practitioners* — JNP (Volume 7, Issue 1, January 2011), http://www.sowashco.org/files/department/nutrition/The%20Surprising%20Benefits%20of%20the%20Family%20Meal.pdf

Zhou, Xinyue, 'Those Were the Days: Counteracting Loneliness with Nostalgia', *Association for Psychological Science*, 1 October 2008, https://www.psychologicalscience.org/news/releases/those-were-the-days-counteracting-loneliness-with-nostalgia.html

O'Neill, Nathalie, 'Feeling Alone? Indulge in Some Nostalgia, the New Cure for Loneliness', Bustle.com, 9 July 2013, https://www.bustle.com/articles/1501-feeling-alone-indulge-in-some-nostalgia-the-new-cure-for-loneliness

Mayo Clinic, 'Forgiveness: Letting go of Grudges and Bitterness', 11 November 2014, http://www.mayoclinic.org/healthy-lifestyle/adult-health/in-depth/forgiveness/art-20047692

Rutledge, Renee, 'You can Save Three Lives With One Blood Donation', http://blog.stridehealth.com/post/save-3-lives-with-1-blood-donation

Blood Source, 'Donate Blood: Blood Facts and Frequently Asked Questions', http://www.bloodsource.org/Donate/Blood-Facts-FAQs

Christakis, Nicholas, Sociology, Harvard University, 'The Social Contagion of Generosity', Science of Generosity, University of Notre Dame, http://generosityresearch.nd.edu/current-research-projects/christakis/

Romm, Aviva, 'The Science Is In: To Boost Your Immune System, Give, Connect & Hug', Aviva Romm, 23 December 2014, https://avivaromm.com/love-boosts-immunity/

Parker-Pope, Tara, 'The Cure for Exhaustion? More Exercise', *The New York Times*, 29 February 2008,
https://well.blogs.nytimes.com/2008/02/29/the-cure-for-exhaustion-more-exercise/

Harvard Medical School, 'Walking: Your Steps to Health', *Harvard Health Publications*, August 2009, https://www.health.harvard.edu/newsletter_article/Walking-Your-steps-to-health

LaCroix, A. Z., Leveille, S. G., Hecht, J. A., Grothaus, L. C. and Wagner, E. H. March 1996, 'Does Walking Decrease the Risk of Cardiovascular Disease Hospitalizations and Death in Older Adults?' *Journal of the American Geriatrics Society*, 44. 113-20. 10.1111/j.1532-5415.1996.tb02425.x, https://www.researchgate.net/publication/14623039_Does_Walking_Decrease_the_Risk_of_Cardiovascular_Disease_Hospitalizations_and_Death_in_Older_Adults

Walker, K., Piers, L., Putt, R., Jones, J. and O'Dea, K, American Diabetes Association vol. 22 no. 4 555–561, 1 April 1999, 'Effects of Regular Walking on Cardiovascular Risk Factors and Body Composition in Normoglycemic Women and Women with Type 2 Diabetes', http://care.diabetesjournals.org/content/22/4/555.article-info

Walking for Health, 'Preventing illness',
https://www.walkingforhealth.org.uk/get-walking/why-walk/healthy-bodies/preventing-illness

Age UK, 'Walk Your Way to Health', Updated 22 May 2017, http://www.ageuk.org.uk/health-wellbeing/keeping-fit/walk-your-way-to-health/how-walking-can-improve-your-health/

Groundology: Scientific Research, http://www.groundology.co.uk/scientific-research

Shinrin-yoku, the medicine of being in the forest, http://www.shinrin-yoku.org/

Bruno S Frey, Christine Benesch & Alois Stutzer, 'Does Watching TV Make us Happy?' *Journal of Economic Psychology*, 2007, vol. 28, issue 3, pages 283–313

R. Douglas Fields, 'Does TV Rot Your Brain?' *Scientific American Mind*, 1 January 2016, https://www.scientificamerican.com/article/does-tv-rot-your-brain/

Knapton, Sarah, 'Fasting for Three Days Can Regenerate Entire Immune System, Study Finds', *The Telegraph*, 5 June 2014, http://www.telegraph.co.uk/science/2016/03/12/fasting-for-three-days-can-regenerate-entire-immune-system-study/

Harvard Medical School, 'The Sweet Danger of Sugar', *Harvard Health Publications*, May 2017, https://www.health.harvard.edu/heart-health/the-sweet-danger-of-sugar

Body Ecology, 'The 25 Key Reasons You Want to Dramatically Reduce or Avoid Sugar in Your Diet', https://bodyecology.com/articles/25_reasons_to_avoid_sugar.php

Kanz, Fabian, Medical University of Vienna, 'Roman Gladiators Ate a Mostly Vegetarian Diet and Drank a Tonic of Ashes After Training', *ScienceDaily*, 20 October 2014, https://www.sciencedaily.com/releases/2014/10/141020090006.htm

Gaidos, Susan, 'The Secret to Memory? A Good Night's Sleep', *Society for Neuroscience*, 3 March 2015, http://www.brainfacts.org/sensing-thinking-behaving/sleep/articles/2015/the-secret-to-memory-a-good-nights-sleep/

Gillman, Steve, 'Ten Amazing Brain Facts', 180 Technology Tips, 2006, http://www.180techtips.com/article6.htm

Begley, Sharon, 'The Brain: How the Brain Rewires Itself', *Time*, 19 January 2017, http://content.time.com/time/magazine/article/0,9171,1580438-2,00.html

Jarrett, Christian, 'All You Need To Know About the 10 Percent Brain Myth, in 60 Seconds', *Wired*, 24 July 2014, https://www.wired.com/2014/07/everything-you-need-to-know-about-the-10-brain-myth-explained-in-60-seconds/

Levitin, Daniel, 'This is Your Brain on Music', Atlantic Books, 1 May 2008

Learner, Sue, 'Therapeutic Gardening Boosts Wellbeing in Care Homes', Carehome.co.uk, 3 August 2015, https://www.carehome.co.uk/news/article.cfm/id/1570297/therapeutic-gardening-boosts-wellbeing-care-homes

Greenpeace USA, 'Save the Bees', http://www.greenpeace.org/usa/sustainable-agriculture/save-the-bees/

Shankar Mahadevan Academy, 'Ten Reasons Why Everyone Should Learn To Play Musical Instrument', 13 March 2013, http://www.shankarmahadevanacademy.com/blog/Ten-Reasons-Why-Everyone-Should-Learn-To-Play-Musical-Instrument

Anita Collins, 'How Playing an Instrument Benefits Your Brain', TED Ed Lesson, 22 July 2014

Williams, Ray, 'How Workplace Happiness Can Boost Productivity', 20 July 2010, https://www.psychologytoday.com/blog/wired-success/201007/how-workplace-happiness-can-boost-productivity

Caprino, Kathy, 'How Happiness Directly Impacts Your Success', *Forbes*, 6 June 2013, https://www.forbes.com/sites/kathycaprino/2013/06/06/how-happiness-directly-impacts-your-success/#1511437618bc

Phegan, Barry, Ph.D, '141 — The Benefits of a Good Organization Culture', Company Culture,
http://companyculture.com/141-the-benefits-of-a-good-organization-culture/

Brown, Joel, 'Benjamin Franklin's Daily Schedule For Success', 28 December 2013, https://addicted2success.com/success-advice/benjamin-franklins-daily-schedule-for-success/

Alban, Deane, '15 Brain Exercises to Keep Your Mind Sharp', Be Brain Fit, https://bebrainfit.com/brain-exercises/

Acknowledgements

From the bottom of my heart, thank you **Oli**, my co-Author, for always being there. **Martin**, you deserve a very big, special thanks. Your positive energy, love for life, care for people and faith in me helped bring this book out into the world. I will always be indebted to you. You are a true gentleman and one of the most inspiring men I have ever met. Thank you **Carla**, for giving me the inspiration for this book and for always being a true, supportive friend. **Ruth**, thank you for your valued input into the development of this book. You have the most beautiful heart of gold. **Hayley**, thanks for being the best Route 66 driving buddy and for your unshakeable belief in me. You always know just what to say. **Jo**, thank you for a lifetime of memories together since we were three years old. You're the best friend a girl could have. **Dag**, you are my kindred spirit. Thank you for being there for me, understanding me and loving me for me. Thank you **Balinda**, for your many wonderful ideas and helping me visualise the book. Thank you **Helen** and **Madeleine**, for providing valuable insight and positive contributions at just the right time. Thank you **Lyanne**, for being one of the most thoughtful people I know. You're always close to my heart no matter where in the world you are. Thank you **Mum, Dad, James, Sarah, Daniel and Thomas** for the unconditional love and support you give me; and my close friends, **Hannah, Sophie, Sam, Laura, Cez, Carly, Nicky, Louise** and **Gem**. You're the reason I am who I am and you all have a special place in my heart. Finally a big thank you **Matt**, for giving me the guidance and last little push to make this happen.

Thank you to ALL my **friends, family and everyone** who I have met in my life for giving me inspiration for this book. You are proof that the world is full of good people.

Laura

First and foremost, I am most grateful to **Laura**. She embodies the spirit of this book and she is the one who made it happen. I am privileged to call her my friend. A huge debt of gratitude is also due to **Martin**. We shall never know where this book might have been without him. He provided drive and inspiration at a critical time and we can never repay him for all he has done and continues to do. Thank you to **Vicki** and **Lily** and all my **family and friends** for their love and support.

Finally, a sincere thanks to **everyone** who reads and enjoys this book; it was for you that we wrote it. I wish you all peace, happiness and love.

Oliver

About The Authors

Laura Sharp: I was born on 8th October 1983 in Northampton, England. I love doing yoga and meditation, seeing new places and trying new things. I have been writing my own Birthday List every year since my mid-twenties. A long-term goal of mine has always been to write a book and get it published and what better topic than that of something that has enriched my life. I hope this book will inspire others and make people smile.

Oliver North: I was born in Northampton, England in the early 1980s. I am a passionate reader, predominantly on topics including philosophy, history, investigative journalism and the meaning of life. Laura and I have known each other since we were 17 and working on this book together has enriched our already strong friendship. In my opinion, The Birthday List is a force for good and I believe it is a perfect time to let the world see it and benefit from its positivity. From my personal research and experience, I can only conclude that the meaning of life is to learn and to grow. This book is a map to doing just that.